Covering the
Community

◆　　◆　　◆

Pine Forge Press Titles of Related Interest

Second Thoughts: Conventional Wisdom Through the Sociological Eye, 2nd. Ed. by Karen Cerulo and Janet Ruane

Media/Society: Industries, Images, and Audiences, 2nd Ed. by David Croteau and William Hoynes

Crime and Everyday Life: Insights and Implications for Society, 2nd Ed. by Marcus Felson

Exploring Social Issues Using SPSS for Windows 95/98 by Joseph F. Healey, John Boli, Earl Babbie, and Fred Halley

Sociology: Exploring the Architecture of Everyday Life (text), 2nd Ed. by David Newman

Sociology: Exploring the Architecture of Everyday Life (readings), 2nd Ed. by David Newman

Building Community: Social Science in Action by Philip Nyden, Anne Figert, Mark Shibley, and Darryl Burroughs

The McDonaldization of Society, Rev. Ed. by George Ritzer

Shifts in the Social Contract: Understanding Change in American Society by Beth Rubin

Sociology for a New Century: A Pine Forge Press Series
Edited by Charles Ragin, Wendy Griswold, and Larry Griffin

Crime and Disrepute by John Hagan

An Invitation to Environmental Sociology by Michael M. Bell

Global Inequalities by York Bradshaw and Michael Wallace

Schools and Societies by Steven Brint

How Societies Change by Daniel Chirot

Ethnicity and Race: Making Identities in a Changing World by Stephen Cornell and Doug Hartmann

The Sociology of Childhood by William A. Corsaro

Cultures and Societies in a Changing World by Wendy Griswold

Gods in the Global Village: The World's Religions in Sociological Perspective by Lester R. Kurtz

Waves of Democracy: Social Movements and Political Change by John Markoff

Development and Social Change: A Global Perspective by Philip McMichael

Constructing Social Research by Charles C. Ragin

Women and Men at Work by Barbara Reskin and Irene Padavic

Cities in a World Economy by Saskia Sassen

Gender, Family, and Social Movements by Suzanne Staggenborg

Covering the Community:
A Diversity Handbook
for Media

Leigh Stephens Aldrich

PINE FORGE PRESS, INC.

Thousand Oaks • London • New Delhi

For information:

 Pine Forge Press
2455 Teller Road
Thousand Oaks, California 91320
(805) 499-4224
E-mail: sales@pfp.sagepub.com

SAGE Publications Ltd.
6 Bonhill Street
London EC2A 4PU
United Kingdom

SAGE Publications India Pvt. Ltd.
M-32 Market
Greater Kailash I
New Delhi 110 048 India

Production Coordinator: Windy Just
Production Editor: Wendy Westgate
Designer/Typesetter: Marion Warren
Cover: Ravi Balasuriya
Indexer: Jean Casalegno

Printed in the United States of America

Library of Congress Cataloging-in-Publication Data

Aldrich, Leigh Stephens.
    Covering the community: A diversity handbook for media/by
Leigh Stephens Aldrich.
        p. cm.—(A diversity stylebook for media)
    Includes bibliographical references (p.) and index.
    ISBN 0-7619-8513-1 (acid-free paper)
    1. Mass media and culture—Handbooks, manuals, etc.
    2. Pluralism (Social sciences)—Handbooks, manuals, etc.
    I. Title. II. Series.
    P94.6.A43   1999
    302.23—dc21   98-58151

TO SHIRLEY BIAGI
Mentor and Friend

About the Author

LEIGH STEPHENS ALDRICH is Professor of Journalism and Communication Studies at California State University, Sacramento. She is the author of more than 500 articles, studies and desktop study guides. Her book, *12 Steps to Clear Writing,* won a National Federation of Press Women first place instructional book award. In her business consulting work she has trained thousands of people in communications. She is a Fellow of the Poynter Institute for Media Studies.

About the Publisher

Pine Forge Press is an educational publisher, dedicated to publishing innovative books and software throughout the social sciences. On this and any other of our publications, we welcome your comments and suggestions.
Please write to:

Pine Forge Press
A Sage Publications Company
2455 Teller Road
Thousand Oaks, CA 91320
(805) 499-4224
E-Mail: sales@pfp.sagepub.com

Visit our World Wide Web site, your direct link to a multitude of online resources: www.pineforge.com

Contents

Preface

———————◆———————

Today, as never before, it is important for media to have some guidance in reporting and showing the diverse communities that make up the nation. This handbook should be useful in print and broadcast newsrooms across the country, and it should be required for journalism and communication studies instructors and students. Issues of race, gender and class are discussed. Research and preferences come directly from community groups that represent our American society.

Covering the Community is meant to stand alone as a textbook, or it can be used as a supplemental text. It was written to be a companion book to *The Associated Press Stylebook and Manual*. AP style is used for the most part throughout the book so that students and professionals can read in the style in which they are accustomed to writing.

Chapters explain the importance of diversity in journalism, photography and graphics. The first half of the book is a "how-to" guide for identifying and writing diversity stories, beginning with newspapers. The next few chapters introduce issues and solutions in photography, television, radio, public relations and advertisements. The last part of the book is devoted to resources, with an example of a diversity story and a glossary of preferred terms. The exercises included in the book can introduce students to diversity and its effect on media and offer an opportunity for students to practice diversity in reporting.

Testing this book's material in the newsroom and in the classroom will be the wellspring of evaluation. We welcome your comments as a guide for future editions. Thank you for choosing *Covering the Community*.

LEIGH STEPHENS ALDRICH
StephensLF@aol.com
California State University, Sacramento

◆

Acknowledgments with Appreciation

This book is the result of contributions from many who are interested in the diverse community in which we live. I want to thank Shirley Biagi and Ginny McReynolds for their thorough edit of the manuscript and for their support throughout the project. A special thank-you to my husband Bob Aldrich, an enthusiastic motivator and tireless researcher. Dr. Virginia Kidd, Suzanne Sommer, Cari Vinci, Christina Navarette, Lisa Trask, Reagan Wisham, and Jay Wisham all gave professional and personal inspiration throughout the work.

My California State University, Sacramento students and State Hornet staff taught me the meaning of diversity. Our students' courage and success such as that of Giselle Fernandez and Joan Lunden have inspired me throughout the years to continue working on diversity and women's issues.

A special thank-you to the professionals who made this book possible: Pine Forge Press Publisher Stephen Rutter, his assistant Jean Skeels, Wendy Westgate, Windy Just, David Nakamura, Art Nauman, Stephen Magagnini, Jade Moon, Kenneth F. Irby, Valerie Hyman, Don Fry, Roy Peter Clark,

Joyce Mitchell, Dr. Ann L. Gerhardt, Dr. Ray Oshiro, Dr. Robert Humphrey, Marilyn Kern-Foxworth, Larry Dalton, Kit Cullen and Elaine Hussey. My deepest appreciation to the reviewers who molded the book and pushed my writing and editing skills to the limit:

Brenda Dervin, *Ohio State University*
Victoria Goff, *University of Wisconsin, Green Bay*
Lauren Kessler, *University of Oregon*
Catherine Mitchell, *University of North Carolina, Asheville*
Barbara Straus Reed, *Rutgers University*
Pamela Shoemaker, *Syracuse University*
Antone Silvia, *University of Rhode Island*
Carol Stepp, *University of Maryland, College Park*
Bernell Tripp, *University of Florida*

1 Examining Diversity

Throughout the book, certain terms will be interchangeable. In the spirit of the book topic, we asked when we were unsure of what to call certain groups. Chapter 9, "Going to the Source," explains reasons we found for terms used for different ethnic groups. For example, *The Associated Press Stylebook and Libel Manual* uses the term *black,* not *African American* (Goldstein, 1998). *Black* covers a broader group, including American-born blacks, recent African immigrants, Haitians and Jamaicans. We use both terms and use the exact terms interviewees used. Some newer textbooks are using *African American,* yet the leading journalists organizations are named the National Association of Black Journalists and the National Black Media Coalition.

Native American is used for *American Indian.* Some newspapers have returned to using *American Indian* as distinguished from *Asian Indian.* The professional journalists organization is the Native American Journalists Association.

Hispanic is broad-based and covers numerous ethnic groups, whereas *Latino* generally means those from the Latin American countries. *Mexican American* or *Puerto Rican* is more specific and preferred. Many Mexican Americans use the term *Chicano* also. The journalists organization is named the National Association of Hispanic Journalists.

It is obvious the book cannot meet all needs, but we tried to use all acceptable terms. The fact is that terms change with the times and with social drama. The job now is yours, to ask your story subjects what they would like to be called if the story requires an ethnic identification.

———————————◆———

The social climate in the 21st century makes the job of reporting difficult. Journalists, covering local, national and global strife, struggle to report as fairly as possible on issues such as ethnic cleansing, government raids on religious sect compounds and gang drive-by shootings.

Media develop stories daily on political, religious and lifestyle differences, and many stories report urban struggles among groups within the community. Many issues involve fairness, accuracy and ethics, while giving readers and viewers a news picture from which to make up their own minds about the events.

The Importance of Covering the Community

Today's reporters need to understand differences. Print and broadcast reporters must be able to confront a story, armed with open minds and a willingness to listen. They must be equipped with adequate language and the symbols of our culture to report American diversity and to cover the community. Additionally, the imagemakers, photographers and graphic designers especially need sensitivity to the community images they present to the public.

Care should be taken to emphasize the community and to support community harmony. Yet, communities exist within communities. Although American differences make America interesting and strong, an overlying theme should be respect for differences and support for unity as Americans. This country weaves a patchwork quilt with millions of pieces that make up the whole. Each piece shows uniqueness, with varying colors, textures and sizes. Yet, the strength of the quilt unifies the pieces.

Keith B. Richburg (1997), a black American who runs *The Washington Post*'s Hong Kong bureau, says, "Having seen in Africa what tribal hatreds can do, I believe that separation is the wrong approach. There's no point in talking about going 'back' to anywhere, in finding missing 'roots.' Far better that we all put our energies into making America work better, into realizing the dream of a multiracial society, than into clinging to the myth that we belong anyplace else."

The Importance of Diversity in the Newsroom

One of the major issues media need to address is to diversify their staffs. Women and minorities have had a hard time making in-roads into positions in newspapers, radio, and television. The numbers are slowly rising, but there is not a close population reflection in reporters, editors and news managers.

David Nakamura, a *Washington Post* writer, covers Maryland sports for the *Post*. He is the son of a Jewish mother and a Japanese father. He says he thinks journalists meet their greatest obstacles in the newsroom. Because there are few Asian athletes, he says he faces discrimination in getting assignments. The stereotype is "Asians don't get involved in sports." He says that many times he is the only Asian in the news box at a sports event. Although he usually covers Maryland sports, he was sent to Washington, D.C. to cover the "Million Man March."

"I find that discrimination uses code phrases," he says. "Rather than telling white men applying for media jobs, 'You're just not a good enough writer,' those hiring say, 'Well, you're a white man, and we have to hire minorities.' This makes white men hate minorities"(D. Nakamura, 1995).

Nakamura, a graduate of the University of Missouri, was hired by the *Post* in 1994. He encourages minority students to take internships to get a foot in the door. He says he believes internships are essential to new journalists and encourages them to apply for as many as they can afford to take. Some are paid and others unpaid; the student usually has to fund some of his or her expenses. Nakamura says students should apply early because large newspapers start recruiting for summer interns in November of the year before.

Defining Diversity

Diversity describes an environment, such as a community, that includes representation of multiple groups. Diversity places an emphasis on accepting and respecting differences by recognizing that no one group is intrinsically superior to the other.

Reporting events involving this diverse population takes skill and sensitivity to differences. Not until the 20th century did the idea emerge that immigrants could serve the country best by keeping their identity and by enriching the culture of the whole with their special contributions. Reporting without bias can be achieved by paying attention to these contributions.

Journalists should also carefully consider the following elements when writing.

1. **Choose the right word** and remember the English language is ever-changing, colorful and rich in nuances and connotations.
2. **Avoid stereotypes.** In reporting the news, journalists should not use words that demean or trivialize any group. Endeavor to include differences in reporting a news event.
3. **Don't omit.** This denigrates diverse people and groups when media stories cover predominantly white males.

Because today's majority will be tomorrow's minority, journalists cannot limit reporting the world through a male, European heritage perspective. The yardstick for any story should embody a separate measure of the news event and positive differences of the people involved.

Scholar Jean Gaddy Wilson says, "Our goal should be to provide an inclusive, nonbiased and nonjudgmental language that reflects today's reality. By eliminating both blatant and subtle sexism, racism, ageism and other stereotypes from our writing and speech, we actually provide a more reliable, credible look at today's culture" (Brooks, Pinson and Wilson, 1997).

This country's history of slavery and suppression of gender and minority rights leaves us with a language that diminishes the roles of women and minorities. It leaves us with a powerful root system of bias that is going to take some time and sensitivity to change.

When speaking to Unity '94 delegates, Dorothy Gilliam, a *Washington Post* columnist and former president of the National Association of Black Journalists, said, "A media that does not reflect its community eventually will not survive."

Unity '94 brought together a convention of four separate organizations: the National Association of Black Journalists, the National Association of Hispanic Journalists, the Asian American Journalists Association and the Native American Journalists Association. The next convention meets in 1999.

Evelyn Hsu, a *Washington Post* editor and former president of the Asian American Journalists Association, pointed out at the convention, "Our common goal is to have better portrayals of our community. . . . Our message to the industry is that diversity is better for the product. . . . Having people with divergent backgrounds helps give you a richer product."

A Unity-sponsored study done at San Francisco State University found that in photos, through headlines and in news footage African Americans are often portrayed as "rap stars, drug addicts (or) welfare mothers," while Latinos are portrayed as "aliens and foreigners." Asian Americans are seen as "inscrutable, manipulative" invaders of U.S. business, and Native Americans are seen as "Indian drunks"(*News Watch*, 1994).

Developing Awareness

Communication studies show that changes in attitude about different groups are brought about by sharing information, reducing uncertainty and building trust. People who encounter a belief that they think is harmful will not change that belief easily, nor should they. What journalists must do is develop an awareness of differences.

Everyone screens others though a cultural bias; therefore, it is necessary to *understand your own beliefs* before understanding that others have a right to their differences. Journalists, writers, photographers and imagemakers can work on understanding that different values, attitudes and styles of communication are not necessarily bad or inferior, just different.

Listening is the key to cross-cultural communication. Journalists can *develop active listening skills* to learn about the needs and the cultures of others. Paying attention to word usage and different meanings attached to words will benefit the writer. You might say that each special group has a jargon of its own, and sometimes those words are used in a way that the mainstream press misunderstands.

For example, a television journalist in the Midwest described how she met a friend she had not seen for months. The friend asked her how things were down at the TV station. The friend did not know the station had gone out of business. The journalist explained the station had "gone to black," which is TV talk for end of story. A few sentences later in the conversation, the friend asked the journalist how it was working for all black management.

Identifying "Ism"s

For journalists to identify every "ism" is impossible, yet there are blatant examples that can be a beginning point of identification. *Racism, sexism, ageism* and *classism* are some that insult and limit the potential of many special groups. These "ism"s are demonstrated in word choices, stereotypes or typecasting and in omission.

Words convey values, opinions and beliefs. Words can objectively report, or they can show bias and hatred. For example, after cartoonist Dennis Renault of *The Sacramento Bee* used the word "nigger" in a cartoon on the editorial page in the February 4, 1994 edition, community response was loud and vocal (Alim, 1994). Although Renault's intent was satirical, the cartoon was taken another way by the black community. (See Chapter 6 for discussion.)

Stereotypes, which bring to mind a derogatory image, are quick picture messages that tell readers, listeners or viewers how they should think about an individual or group. Media use stereotypes as a shorthand to get instant attention. Advertisements show stereotypes, and so do cartoons. Of course, there is nothing wrong with a quick image unless it demeans a person or a special group.

For example, the dumb, blonde sexy image of a female "decorating" a refrigerator or an automobile limits the way the reader or viewer thinks about women. This says blondes are not intelligent, women use sex to manipulate, women should be used to sell products and sex comes when you buy the product. This, translated into daily lives, affects the way employers view and hire blondes and all women, how employers think women should be treated, and ultimately, how they think they should be paid.

Omission of an individual or special group that should be represented is perhaps the largest "ism" that can be identified. Since minorities and women are many times excluded from mainstream news and prime-time news, readers and viewers don't think about them not being there. What effect could this have on culture? If we don't see African American doctors, disabled people actively participating in sports, Mexican American CEOs, gay, fundamentalist ministers or women mathematicians, how will we ever envision those groups taking part in all segments of life? These people do exist, but rarely does the public get a glimpse of them through mainstream media

Following are some "ism"s that media reflect.

Sexism is an "ism." Women are making progress in some areas, but they must be represented more equally to break down stereotypes that have existed for centuries. Some of these stereotypes are: Women are not strong. Women have emotional problems related to their reproductive organs. Women are just not suited to some professions. Additionally, these stereotypes imply that only women should be in the home, taking care of the children. These images limit jobs and life potential for women.

Male bashing demonstrates a swing in the opposite direction, and many men are tired of being the object of sexism. For example, stereotypes exist that men should be macho, protect females and show little emotion. Many believe men do not love their children as deeply as women because of the image of the absentee father. Beliefs such as these have created a chasm within male-female relationships. These concepts are sexist and just as damaging to men as images that are racist or ageist.

Homophobia contributes to strident criticism of homosexuals, male or female. Although some experts say homosexuality is a lifestyle choice, a number of credible studies point to homosexuality as a biological fact. This in turn equates to discrimination toward a person because he or she is born with a certain trait, such as blue eyes.

The AIDS epidemic has hit a large population in the male, gay community. Journalists reporting on this segment of the population and reporting on HIV-positive individuals should present the stories as sensitively as possible to avoid further discrimination of the group. AIDS is not just a problem for gays. The World Health Organisation estimates that by the year 2000, 40 million people will be infected with HIV globally (Centers for Disease Control and Prevention, May 20, 1996).

Racism is the belief that certain races are superior to others. This tends to contribute to the fact that society then grants special status to certain races. This belief system advocates a separation from that "inferior" group or groups, and sometimes promotes violence toward that group. This is true of cultural and ethnic differences also. With race and cultural bias xenophobia adds to the complex issues relating to differences among people. *Xenophobia* is a fear or hatred of strangers or foreigners (Hussey, 1994).

Journalists must report on geographic bias that exists worldwide. Recent conflicts in Bosnia, Croatia, Somalia, Iraq and Afghanistan bring to the forefront that racial, cultural, ethnic and religious differences intermingle to create problems people have not learned to deal with peacefully.

Characteristics of culture are vast, and people are intolerant of religions, dialects, gestures, dress, eating habits, time consciousness or lack of it, group values and work habits. When media report these elements of race and culture, they should seek perspective from within the specific group to explain the news story in its context.

Social scientists agree that one reason why people hold prejudice is because of a lack of understanding. Many newspapers are creating positions called, "the ethnic beat" or "the cultural beat" to be more sensitive to community differences. Murray Dubin, reporter for the *Philadelphia Inquirer*, created one of the country's first ethnic beats in 1986.

Physical prejudice exists among people surrounding *ageism, youthism, sizeism* and *disabilities*. The term *geezer bashing* has come to describe blaming the aging population for the economic drain on the country through Social Security. Additionally, older employees have been laid off from their jobs early to make way for younger, cheaper employees. American culture shows little respect for aging.

GUIDELINES FOR
REPORTING DIVERSITY

1. When practical and relevant to the story, ask those involved in the story how they want to be identified.
2. Identify your own biases. Are they getting in the way of the story?
3. Don't reinforce cultural assumptions and stereotypes. Avoid omission.
4. Be aware that colloquial expressions may be verbally acceptable but not acceptable in print unless they are needed in quotations.
5. Go where the people are. Attend cultural awareness workshops. Volunteer with special groups so you can understand their day-to-day problems. Go to their meetings. Go to foreign film festivals.
6. Don't sensationalize a story, using cultural biases (i.e., highlighting a mixed marriage), unless it is relevant to the story.
7. Although the scoop is desirable, accuracy is more desirable. Don't jump to conclusions just to get the story first. Don't speculate what might happen because people form opinions from your speculations.
8. Don't always tell the story through the white male perspective. Put yourself in the shoes of your interviewees. How would you like to be reported?
9. Always talk with representatives of both sides of the issue. Use balance in presenting different voices within your story.
10. Be a good storyteller. Put your reader into the story by showing sensory details: *the black armband, the smell of curry, the touch of the older woman's cold, wrinkled hand.*
11. Develop sources within special groups. They can get you inside the story.
12. Work on being nonthreatening. Tell your interviewees they are doing you a favor by talking with you, and they will help the public better understand their group: religious, racial, ethnic, gender and age.
13. Find and nurture sources among many local and national racial, ethnic and special interest groups. For example, *USA Today* has developed a source book that aids reporters in understanding the different segments of the population among their readership.
14. Talk with people in their own territory so they feel more comfortable.
15. Clean up quotes unless the story is about language. Don't publicly embarrass innocent interviewees.

Prejudice against people who are overweight can take the form of job discrimination. Women are particular targets of weight control programs that are advertised endlessly. Current scientific studies report that genetics have a great deal to do with a person's size. This weight phobia is a cultural bias perpetuated by media that makes no allowance for a 200-pound woman or a 130-pound man. Both are discriminated against. Large women are considered lazy, sloppy and unproductive. Small men are considered sexually inadequate and wimps to be picked on. In the workplace these prejudices can translate into less pay and less promotion—or worse, rejection for employment.

People with disabilities have become quite vocal. Recent changes in American Sign Language point out that people who cannot hear may be more sensitive to the diverse issues around human differences.

Interestingly, Professor Elissa Newport, a University of Rochester psychologist, says, "In American Sign Language, politically incorrect terms are often a visual representation of the ugly metaphors we have about people" (*The New York Times*, January 3, 1994).

In recent years, a hearing-impaired person would sign the word "Japanese" simply by twisting the little finger next to the eye. Now American Sign Language users avoid this because it makes a graphic reference to a stereotypical physical feature. Instead, they press the thumb and index fingers of both hands together and pull them apart, carving the silhouette of Japan in the air.

Occupational prejudice is sometimes subtle. Wrapped up in this category are elitism, class and caste systems, all supporting power and money. Some young people turn down McBurger jobs because they pay minimum wage and because society makes fun of the jobs. Others discriminated against are store workers such as those who work at McMart, garbage collectors, janitors, waitresses, itinerant farm workers and house cleaners. Many people who are clustered in these jobs are the disenfranchised: the poor and uneducated.

Because Americans are diverse, journalists, photojournalists, public relations practitioners and mass media have the task of understanding and interpreting the vast world that exists.

Gerald M. Sass, former senior vice president of The Freedom Forum, said, "We make progress through people, not programs. That's people first. Second, there's no progress without some abrasiveness. Third, there's no progress without risk" (Sass, July 28, 1994).

WORKING THE BEAT

Exercises

1. List on a piece of paper all the *special interest groups* to which you belong, such as race, ethnic group, geographic group, religious group, gender and class. Also list physical traits that describe you such as disabled, overweight or unattractive by media beauty standards. Discuss: Has anyone in the class never felt any prejudice because of belonging to at least one of these groups? What do you think causes people to show discrimination? Discuss how you can work on this as it relates to your writing and reporting?

2. List all the derogatory words, phrases, stereotypes and assumptions you can think of pertaining to one of the special groups you listed you belong to in Exercise 1. Pair off within the classroom and share your list with your partner. Discuss and ask your partner if he or she knows anything else to add to your list. How do you feel when you see this list? Discuss in class. Are you surprised at some of the words and stereotypes to which others object?

3. Clip five articles about at least three different diversity groups. Analyze these articles. Were the groups and individuals portrayed fairly? Was the whole story told? What would you have done differently if you had written these stories?

4. Nonverbal communication is 93 percent of the total. Choose a classmate you do not know as a partner. Allowing 5 minutes total, introduce yourself to your partner without using any words. What did you learn? What were your similarities? Your differences? How does observation play an essential part in reporting a story about diversity and women?

5. For the following story, write a newspaper headline, the lead and the nut graph (a sentence that states the main focus of the story), using two different viewpoints: first write the story from an economically well-off, white male perspective; next write the story from a black female perspective— a woman who lives in that neighborhood.

Story Facts:

♦ Two black teenaged males were killed Sunday at 4 p.m. in a shoot-out in Pine Park, which is within a poor, diversely populated neighborhood. The police suspect drugs are at the core of the dispute.

♦ Businesses in the area are suffering from the crime-ridden neighborhood.

WORKING THE BEAT (continued)

- ◆ The Chamber of Commerce has pumped $50,000 into the area to boost business.
- ◆ At least 15 other teens were in the park Sunday when the two youths were killed.
- ◆ Because of past violence, neighborhood mothers have formed a mother's club. Ironically, they were meeting at the time of the deaths.
- ◆ Fill in any story details you need to write the story from the two perspectives.

Who would you interview for quotes and information? Where would you get background information about the neighborhood? How are your story angles different? Should they be different? How do race and special interests enter into this situation?

2 Preparing for a Diarsity Story

◆——————————

Preparing for the diversity story includes all the techniques of preparing for any news story. First, there must be "news." News is a report of a recent event. For example, "A five-alarm fire destroyed most of the old Wells Fargo building in downtown Fremont early today." A diversity angle might be that the building had been donated for use by the community as a rehabilitation center for the disabled.

News is also a report of current events, such as the status of a legislative battle over whether gambling should be legalized within the state. A diversity angle might be the response of Native Americans who would feel the competition because of legalized gambling already in operation on reservations.

◆——————————

Identifying Community News Values

The elements of news are focused on currency, timeliness, impact, proximity, prominence, the unusual, controversy or human interest. News is today's information set in world context. News also must be localized to be effective to the reader; it must be in proximity to the reader's life. Celebrities are news, anything novel or unusual is news; and of course, controversy and human interest stories are news.

So if you are writing about the various communities within the larger community of your readership, all the elements of news must still apply. A diversity angle can be considered for every story. In other words, when any news story is prepared, it should pass the test of covering the community—representing the whole community.

▓ Case Study

Principal Buys Uniforms

Jose Risso is the principal of Charles Mack Elementary school in Elk Grove, California. The school introduced a navy-and-white uniform policy, in keeping with parent wishes that the school adopt a dress code.

Principal Risso says, ". . . attendance is up, suspensions are down and behavior has improved noticeably. When you're wearing your uniform, you're doing business—and their business is learning."

The hook of this news story is that Principal Risso is buying clothing for the children out of his own pocket to support this school policy. Charles Mack has the third highest poverty rate in the Elk Grove Unified School District, with half the students coming from families who receive aid to families with dependent children.

The principal said one day he greeted a third-grader with a hand on his shoulder only to discover the child's shirt was wet. The boy said, "Mr. Risso, I washed it . . . and it isn't dry yet."

Risso spent hundreds of his own dollars in the first year of the policy to buy used clothing for the children who have no extra uniforms. He and his wife shop garage sales and thrift shops for white shirts, navy jumpers and slacks for the children. He lobbied the local businesses and community members to donate money for which he was able to purchase 100 new uniforms for students in need. ▓

This story is a community news story of the best kind. It is human interest. It emphasizes the value of uniforms in the education community where gang colors cause violence and where expensive shoes and jackets are stolen for their name brand value.

This story reports on community action pulling citizens together to do something positive for school children. This story also happens to be a diversity story because Jose Risso was born and raised in Peru. When he came to the United States in his late teens, speaking no English, he learned the language through an English immersion program.

Risso received his education through the University of San Francisco and spent 21 years in the classroom before rising to vice principal and principal of a school. He said he felt a need to be a role model for Latino children.

"I want them to think, 'I'm going to grow up to be a principal, or president'" (DeFao, 1997; copyright, *The Sacramento Bee*, 1997). ▨

Testing for Bias

A community story should not contain bias. According to a number of guidelines for writing about diversity, a good test is, "Would I have written about a white male in the same way?" Because the mass media standard for years has been reporting from a white male perspective, it helps to reverse the situation and ask if the story appears biased.

A news service reporting from Wellington, New Zealand carried the headline, *Woman backed as prime minister.* What has gender to do with the qualifications of Jenny Shipley, the new prime minister? She was unanimously approved by a 44-member caucus to lead the country. She *is* the first woman who has been elected prime minister of New Zealand, and this is news, so putting this information in the story is acceptable. But, would you have headlined this story, *Man backed as prime minister?* or *Disabled veteran backed as prime minister?* Probably not.

Additionally, the lead of the story began, *A 45-year-old farmer's wife and former schoolteacher won the ruling party's endorsement today . . .* This lead uses a stereotype of women, introducing her in terms of her relationship to a man; "wife of, sister of, or mother of" (Bee News Service, 1997).

To write without bias, you must be able to identify your own biases. Ask yourself: Have I included any bias related to race, gender, class, age or ethnic descent? Every human being has some kinds of bias against other human beings. What are yours? Only by knowing what they are will you be able to spot them when writing and editing your stories.

Go Where People Live and Work

To write about the community, the reporter must go into the community and get the feel of locations, of cultural differences, of the different sounds and tastes of special groups. Go to cultural gatherings, go into the schools, attend foreign films, ask sources for invitations to weddings, funerals and special holiday celebrations.

Eat the special foods, see the different clothing choices, ask about the cultural history of the clothing and attend religious gatherings. In other words, to understand a special group, immerse yourself in that community.

Ask community sources to explain what you don't understand. Run your information by several people who are knowledgeable about the setting of the community news you are reporting.

Making Ethical Decisions

In every story you write, ethical decisions must be made. Ethics should be considered along with eliminating bias. An ethic is a community code or rule that prescribes behavior in special situations. The reporter must know and consider ethics when writing about the community. Typical ethical questions are: Is it ethical or biased to report on a story where you, the writer, might gain financially by some outcome of the story being published? Are you exploiting any group to report a story?

Ethnic communities complain, with cause, that crime coverage is race based. Melita Garza, ethnic affairs writer for the *Chicago Tribune*,

(text continues on p. 19)

INTERVIEW WITH DIVERSITY
REPORTER STEPHEN MAGAGNINI

Stephen Magagnini of *The Sacramento Bee* carries the title of Senior Writer for Ethnic Affairs and Race Relations. He says Rick Rodriguez, now executive editor of *The Bee,* put him on this beat in late 1993. Enterprise stories make up 95 percent of what he writes. These are stories the reporter generates. (See Magagnini's diversity article in Appendix A.)

"Everybody on the paper should be writing diversity stories, but I'm allowed to concentrate on this," says Magagnini.

He has great enthusiasm for diversity writing and many tips for those writing the stories. When he was working on a story about India's 50-year Independence Day, he talked with five groups: Christians from India, Hindus, Sikhs for and against India and Muslims. He found ideas for four different stories from his interviews.

"I want all the voices in that story from each group. I use outside experts for background. Using only the voices of the story protects against charges of bias," he says. *"This type of story (Independence Day) gives the readers an understanding of the culture and why the people came to California. It's what I'm shooting for in every story, to 'explain and entertain.'"*

It makes it a lot easier for people in a special group to accept criticism if they know the newspaper has been fair in previous informational articles. Magagnini says his approach is to talk with many people within the story and then do background research, such as articles on the Internet.

He says, *"The diversity part of the story can be the hook. A contextual story such as the series I wrote on the Hmong lays the groundwork. I try to give the story voices to those who are least likely to get a voice. I spent a long time researching the shamans, why the Hmong are here, the problems they have, and why they depend on the shaman."*

The shamans are the healers and spiritual leaders. The Hmong are an ethnic group from southern China, Vietnam, Laos and Thailand. Approximately 50,000 came to America as refugees in the mid-1970s, uprooted as a result of a civil war in Laos.

When time came for Magagnini to write the story about 14,000 Hmong being on welfare in Sacramento County, he says they were able to take negative facts because they knew he had been fair about writing about them in the past.

(continued)

INTERVIEW WITH STEPHEN MAGAGNINI (continued)

"The most impact I have is to write a story or series to introduce a group to the readers. First there must be a good story. For example, a Hmong girl fled Fresno and from those who tried to force her to take chemotherapy for ovarian cancer. There was a bitter cultural clash. But I was able to explain the culture through the story."

One year for Martin Luther King Day, Magagnini set out to see what the schools were teaching about King. He says he "found a black kid who does a great imitation of King's 'I Have a Dream' speech all over the country." But what he found was that the youth didn't know much about why the speech was given or why King was so important.

Magagnini says, *"He was a good lead into that story."*

He says, *"Contextual stories do a lot of good. They're worth 20 stories about crime or event news. My goal is twofold: to educate about different groups and to write for groups so they have a living history of their culture. The Hmong shamans may not even exist 30 years from now."*

"My work is not through," says Magagnini. *"At Highlands High School (Northern California), there are 45 different languages spoken."*

STEPHEN MAGAGNINI'S
TIPS FOR DIVERSITY WRITING

1. Talk with many voices within the story.
2. Do background research from articles and experts in the field.
3. Be aware of cultural differences: *"I had a lot of trouble talking with American Indians on the telephone. The Indian way is to meet you face-to-face. When I met them I would say, 'I got your name from so-and-so', and it came out okay."*
4. Don't be put off by discrimination. *"The reporter is going to face discrimination as a reporter no matter where he goes."*
5. Write the lead first, then organize by the key points that stand out in your mind after the interview.
6. Develop many trustworthy sources within each cultural group. Multiply this list by asking, *"Who would agree with you?"* and *"Who doesn't like you?"*
7. For interviews, take a trusted group member with you for language interpretation if needed.
8. Immerse yourself in the culture. Go to their festivals and participate in their customs. Go to conferences and take workshops in diver-

---

INTERVIEW WITH STEPHEN MAGAGNINI (continued)

> sity. *I was in a sweat lodge with Native Americans . . . about 20 Indian people from ages 8 to adult, men and women. It was the most intense experience of my life.*

9. Learn a few words in the language of the people you are interviewing.

> Magagnini says he speaks Italian, Spanish passably, and Mandarin humbly (Magagnini, 1997).

---

tells of a Wisconsin newspaper's Sunday banner headline, "Hispanics More Than Half of All Convicted Drug Felons in Milwaukee."

She says the entire Latino community was outraged because they rarely get much coverage at all, and then there was this story. She says the irony of it was that they were not about to do a story that read, "99 Percent of All White Collar Crime Committed by White Males" (Garza, 1994).

Reporters and editors need to pay attention to these kind of ethical decisions. Keith Woods, editorial writer for the *New Orleans Times-Picayune* says, "It's about time we started asking questions and challenging the ways things are. You've got to express your doubts and passions, and you've got to do it in an environment that will allow for dissent" ("Doing Ethics in Journalism," 1995).

Identifying Sources Within the Community

Every reporter should have a resource list with various sources within the community. Not only should you include the usual experts, such as doctors, engineers and educators, but you should include key community contacts such as a barber, a religious community member, a grocery store clerk, and a city street worker.

"I have a 1,000-inch-long list on my computer of ethnic and racial sources. People I've met on my own and have known over the years," says Stephen Magagnini.

DOING ETHICS

Ask Good Questions to Make Good Ethical Decisions

1. What do I know? What do I need to know?
2. What is my journalistic purpose?
3. What are my ethical concerns?
4. What organizational policies and professional guidelines should I consider?
5. How can I include other people, with different perspectives and diverse ideas, in the decision-making process?
6. Who are the stakeholders—those affected by my decision? What are their motivations? Which are legitimate?
7. What if the roles were reversed? How would I feel if I were in the shoes of one of the stakeholders?
8. What are the possible consequences of my actions? Short term? Long term?
9. What are my alternatives to maximize my truthtelling responsibility and minimize harm?
10. Can I clearly and fully justify my thinking and my decision? To my colleagues? To stakeholders? To the public? ("Doing Ethics in Journalism," 1995)

From videotape, *Doing Ethics in Journalism,* Poynter Institute for Media Studies, St. Petersburg, Florida, 1995. Used with permission.

What is included in this textbook is a guide, but you may have even more diverse groups to cover in your community, and you need to understand them to report accurately and with fairness and balance. The community is just that; it incorporates the rich, the poor, the educated and uneducated, the sick and the well and a wide range of ages and interests.

The National Conference of Christians and Jews and the Asian American Journalists Association in Chicago have published *The Asian American Handbook,* an exceptional model for any group in the nation writing about special groups. Topics include "What It Means to Be Asian American," "Asian American Issues," "Tips for Covering and

Portraying Asian Americans," "Names, Demographics, and a Cultural Observances Listing" (*The Asian American Handbook*, 1991).

As a journalist you can put together your own handbook for all the special groups in your community. This would also be a valuable project for the local Society of Professional Journalists chapter or for the local college journalism department and would benefit media as well as service groups in the community.

Suppose you are preparing a story on Russian immigrants. What would be some considerations when you make the initial contact? Wouldn't it be a valuable piece of information to prepare a cultural profile of the groups within your community?

A CULTURAL PROFILE

Considerations When Interviewing Russians

1. Russians value education for males and females. Even the young can discuss European culture, including art, literature, music and philosophy. Most are at least bilingual, with English being one of the languages.
2. Their heritage of physical suffering and deprivations affects many of their decisions. For example, resources such as food and clothing have been in short supply, which would give them a greater respect for these basics.
3. If you're invited to a Russian home for dinner, it is appropriate to take flowers. Don't, however, take an odd number of blooms because this is considered an omen of a death in the family.
4. Russia has a history of ethnic problems and xenophobia, a distrust of foreigners. There has been anti-Semitic and anti-black discrimination for centuries.
5. They have close family ties and respect the aging. They are doting parents and tend to keep their children physically close to the parents and grandparents.
6. Because of crowding and poverty under communism, the rule per family is usually one or two children.
7. Motherhood is important, as reflected in Russian fairy tales, folklore, art and social structure. Yet, the family tradition is patriarchal.

(continued)

A CULTURAL PROFILE (continued)

8. Russians settling in the United States may have a problem with capitalism because for several generations they have been dependent on government.

9. Under communist rule, women were trained equally and entered all professional fields. With the fall of communism, women's roles are modeling the Western worldview of the woman as homemaker and as sex symbol.

10. Because of its vastness, the former Soviet Union has many religions such as the Russian Orthodox, Roman Catholic, Jewish, Islamic and Buddhist. The aging, particularly older women, kept religion alive during communist rule (Ben, 1995).

Ideas from *Insight Guide: Russia,* Langenscheidt Publishers Inc., 1999. Used with permission.

WORKING THE BEAT

Exercises

1. Make a list of 10 special groups within your own community. Write a cultural profile on each of the 10 groups. What considerations should be made when reporting on them?

2. Identify 10 community sources who are representative of their community but are not the usual media sources.

3. Clip an article about a racial conflict or confrontation. Analyze the article by discussing the situation and the events that led to the current problem. Discuss in class "What causes one group to dislike and distrust another group?" Make a list of steps that could be taken by individuals and communities to encourage racial harmony ("Celebrate Diversity," 1997).

4. Clip five news articles that are diversity stories and analyze them according to bias related to sources. Whom did they use as sources? Whom could they have included as sources? Is community emphasized and separation downplayed?

5. Choose one of the special groups you have identified in Exercise 1 and list 25 locations and events where a reporter could go to understand this special group. Be specific: "The Cypress Lane Day Care Center," "The Buddhist Temple's Annual Bon Dance Celebration," or "Manoa Valley Community Lei Day Festival."

3 Gathering News With a Cultural Spin

◆

The first task of the reporter is to develop news judgment— what is news and what is not. News is a recent event that is of interest to the public. Much writing training focuses on the writer's viewpoint, whereas with news, the focus is on others' viewpoints and interests. Additionally, news stories are backed by facts, not opinions. News writing is writing with a clear purpose, and this is decided by news values.

◆

How to Develop Diversity News Judgment

Diversity reporting is an extra value worth considering for every news story reported. This means making an effort to include the total community. Many newspapers are evolving into what is called "niche" coverage where news is targeted at specific groups. This may have its place in certain areas, but not including the total community leaves the general public in the dark about events and issues that are vital to all.

Journalist Carl Bernstein of Watergate fame highlighted this media problem when he spoke at Boston University in the fall of 1997. He said, "At the heart of the American condition today is the story we've ignored for a generation—race. Race is the most important story in America, straining the fabric of our national existence, touching on all our problems. We're terrified of it, unsure how to begin covering it, and afraid of being incendiary, so we ignore it and the obvious questions.

"Would we permit white people to live by the millions in the hell of our urban housing projects; would we put up with those city school systems if the children trapped in them were white; would we put up with the slaughter by gunfire of white children by the thousand?

"Not for a minute" (Bernstein, September 20, 1997).

Why is it important to the Japanese community to know that African Americans are being "red-lined" for real estate loans? People learn about their world through watching what goes on around them, through watching the activities of others. If you were a Japanese American, looking for your first home, wouldn't it be relevant to you to know that illegal practices are going on related to the planning commission, real estate agents and mortgage lenders in your community?

Wouldn't this be valuable information so you can be cautious that your legal rights are not being denied because you are a minority? Wouldn't this be valuable information so that minority groups could band together to spotlight these illegal practices?

Developing Accuracy, Balance and Fairness, Clarity and Completeness

The highest rule of news is to get it right the first time. Accuracy is most important because lives and businesses can be ruined by misinformation. Not only can your news agency be sued, but legal action and settlement cannot erase the tarnish of wrong information that clings forever to reputation. People look to the news so they can make simple and complex life decisions, from knowing whether to detour around continuing construction to investing thousands of dollars in stock funds.

Joseph Pulitzer once said that the three most important elements in journalism are "Accuracy, accuracy and accuracy"(Laakaniemi, 1995).

Balance and fairness incorporate the fullness of the story. Voices from all sides of an issue should be included. Reporters should attempt to interview opposites sides and include those in the story. Of equal importance is fairness, which is harder to define. But fairness includes major facts, therefore completeness comes into play. A story that includes insignificant information at the expense of significant facts is unfair. It is unfair to mislead or deceive the reader; therefore honesty is extremely important, no matter how distasteful.

The Washington Post Desk Book on Style states, "No story is fair if reporters hide their biases or emotions behind such subtly pejorative words as *refused, despite, admit* and *massive*. So fairness requires straightforwardness ahead of flashiness" (Lippman, 1989).

Clarity should speak for itself, but many times writers sacrifice clarity with poor writing and editing. Never make assumptions about the readers. Explain every detail without belaboring the point. Welcome your editor's comments, for if one person doesn't understand what you're saying, someone in your readership will also misunderstand.

Completeness involves the 5 W's and How. Every story should include *who* is involved and *what* the event is. These are usually the most important and should be put at the top of the lead. Next in importance is the *why* and *how* of the event. Usually last is the *when* and *where*. That means don't begin the lead with the time of day unless the story is about the end of the world being predicted. Then readers want to know when! Don't begin with location (*where*) first unless a nuclear waste leak has occurred, and it is just outside of the city!

Avoid Omission

Journalists are accused of Rolodex interviews—the practice of going back to the few experts for whom they have phone numbers and interviewing them for every story they cover. When watching the news, you get the impression that most experts are the same white males—critics say, "mainly male, mainly pale." How can this omission be avoided?

News agencies can provide a diverse list of experts covering different fields within their community. This, of course, can be updated and rotated. Input from various groups within the community is helpful.

Omission of minorities and women occurs in expert interviews, and it occurs in newsmaking situations. Too many times the news agenda setter chooses the white male as the standard for news and neglects diverse races, ethnic and cultural groups and women. A study, "Names in the News," conducted annually by the Minnesota Women's Press Association, reported that in 1998, women's names appeared in the news about 25 percent of the time. This study was of Minnesota's two largest newspapers.

Study coordinator Jennifer Franklin said, "It will be nearly four decades into the 21st century before women reach parity with men in the news." National media studies confirm this problem (*Media Report to Women*, Spring 1998).

Omission can be described as the more subtle of the elements that make up biased reporting. Leaving out 52 percent of the population and vast numbers of minorities and special groups is a dangerous practice in a democracy. Media should report on all groups. Many think if owners, managers, editors and reporters were more representative of the population, minorities and women would be included in more equal proportion when the news agenda is set.

Sometimes industry fails to show sensitivity. Microsoft Corporation released a thesaurus in a Spanish-language version of the popular Word 6.0 program that offended millions. The thesaurus suggested that *man-eater, cannibal* and *barbarian* could substitute for the Spanish term for *black people*. The program equated *Indians* with *man-eating savages* and offered the Spanish word for *bastard* as a synonym for *people of mixed race*. The term *lesbian* was compared to the words *vicious* and *perverse*. *Occidental*, by contrast, was compared to *white, civilized* and *cultured* (Clark, 1996).

Mass media have the task of providing the news—all the news relevant to the country's vast and diverse population. There is harm in omission. If a Mexican American girl has never seen a female doctor of Mexican descent on television, what are the chances she will dream of becoming one? If an African American boy has never seen a black national prime-time news anchor, what are his chances of ever getting there?

During an exit poll in St. Louis, taken on election day in November 1992, a newscaster outside the polling place spoke with three people, one of whom was wearing a button labeled "Lesbian-Gay activist." That night on the news the other two people were identified by their names and cities of residence, whereas the man with the button was labeled as a "Lesbian-Gay activist."

This incident, says Brad Graham (1996), a gay freelance writer in St. Louis, was "one incident where sexual orientation was not necessarily germane to the story, but it was used as a means of identification."

Media inform, educate, inspire, and they should represent possibilities for life potential to readers and viewers. Not recognizing the needs and realities of the readership could make dramatic changes in the future involving lost revenues and lost audiences. Therefore, accuracy, balance, fairness, clarity and completeness become practical elements.

Cyberspace Is Diverse and Color Blind

Adam Clayton Powell, III (1995) of The Freedom Forum Media Studies Center said, "Open media democratize media, encouraging diversity of all kinds—diversity of content, diversity of opinion, and the full diversity of voices—men and women, young and old, rich and poor, white, black, yellow and brown. Computers are becoming ubiquitous, and if they are open, greater diversity becomes inevitable."

Computer Assisted Journalism (CAJ) is the catch-all term for using computers in news gathering. Computer skills are basic for reporters today. The Internet is a vast collection of computer networks. Millions of users internationally are surfing the Internet.

Nora Paul, the director of news research programs at Poynter Institute for Media Studies, says, "CAJ can be broken down into four R's: Reporting, Research, Reference and Rendezvous. Each of these four functions is critical to news gathering."

She says computers can help reporters conduct their searches, examinations and investigations through the use of spreadsheet programs for complex analysis of large datasets. Reporting relies on primary sources, firsthand, independent or original. It relies on interviews, observations and self-conducted computer analyses.

Research is usually secondary, using databases consisting of reports, articles and studies. Both reporting and research are essential to putting together a full story.

THE GREAT EQUALIZER

In a now-famous *New Yorker* cartoon, a canine sits at a computer. Turning to a companion, the pet brags, "On the Internet, nobody knows you're a dog."

Or white. Or black. Or a woman, a man, in a wheelchair or from California.

. . . *The Internet is truly a medium where, in the words of Martin Luther King, Jr., you can be judged by the content of your character and not by the color of your skin.*

The truth, however, is more complex. The Internet is changing the nature of identity, experts say, but not by making everyone anonymous. Instead, it takes your city, your community and—to a certain extent—your class out of the equation. It erases the boundaries of country, of ghetto, of suburb.

Online there is no "minority" in the conventional sense. Identity is important, but the Internet allows people to interact differently than in the real world. You discover the person before the appearance, for instance, or connect with people who may be minorities in their own community, but majorities in virtual communities (Lynch, 1997).

From "The Great Equalizer," Knight-Ridder News Service, Sept. 17, 1997. Reprinted with permission of Knight-Ridder/Tribune Information Services.

Online services as well as the Internet can put newspapers and magazines ('zines) at your fingertips. A Web search can put you in touch with thousands of sources from the general to the very specific. For example, you might enter "Native American" or "Cherokee Tribe." Cherokee takes you to a web page for the tribe and provides information such as the tribal leaders with their biographies, counties in Oklahoma where most Cherokees live, and the demographics related to each county.

Although, as a student you may be limited in research to the databases offered by the university library or the student newspaper, many other business databases may be used by the newspaper or the television agency you work for in the future. For example, Dun & Bradstreet offers a legal search of public records on businesses in all 50 states, family trees of 200,000 corporations and their subsidiaries, and a Government Activity Report that contains information on businesses, foundations and educational institutions receiving money from the U.S. government (Ullmann, 1995).

The third component in CAJ is reference works, such as dictionaries, encyclopedias, gazetteers, almanacs and glossaries. These are available through the Internet and through CD-ROMs.

The final part of CAJ that Paul says can be helpful to the reporter is rendezvous, or meeting online with experts, other journalists and professional groups. These can be contacted through online services such as America Online or Prodigy. They are also provided through the Internet. You can be in 24-hour contact through e-mail, including list-servers and newsgroups around special topics of interest. On the practical side, remember that anyone in a newsgroup can make an off-the-cuff comment that may not be accurate. Check out the source and check out the information (Paul, 1996).

Finding a Different Angle

Bob Steel, director of ethics at Poynter Institute for Media Studies (1995), says, "You face tough decisions in the field and in the newsroom. You make tough choices that have an impact on people, on the subjects in your stories, on your sources, and on the people in the community who rely on your news gathering skills. Ethics and excellence are inseparable."

Your job as a reporter doesn't only involve reactive response to assignments from your editor, but it involves proactive work to turn up stories that are important to the community. This is where you can be certain you are diversifying the stories you write.

Media experts report that 80 percent of the newspaper stories published are generated by the public, by news and publicity releases. This puts heavy reliance on special interest groups, who may have more money to generate their information than women's or minority groups (Laakaniemi, 1995).

You, as the reporter, have the responsibility to generate stories representative of the diverse population. Where can you get story ideas?

◆ Develop sources and keep a file within the community.

◆ Identify issues that are important to the different commuity groups.

◆ Go into the community and visit hospitals, hospices, clinics, welfare offices, immigration offices, churches, housing and employment organizations that help this community. Observe and listen.

◆ Read about the cultures represented in the community.

◆ Develop a mentor within each culture on whom you can call for information, and who will introduce you to others in that culture.

◆ Read cultural newsletters, newspapers and watch minority television.

◆ Learn the geographical layout of your beat: the names for areas, sections and streets.

For every story you write, there is the untold story you can research. Say you're assigned to cover the story of a 14-year-old girl who abandoned her newborn baby boy in a fast-food restaurant. What kind of follow-up stories could you report? Suppose the girl is Cuban American and unmarried. Suppose the restaurant is in Chinatown. What can you find out about different cultures and their acceptance or nonacceptance of unmarried teen pregnancies? How many unmarried teen mothers are there in the United States? In this community? What kind of help are the different cultural communities offering to these teens? What happens to the babies? What percentage of the babies are of mixed race? What happens to mixed-race babies? Is public welfare supporting these teens? What do community leaders and experts say is the solution to this social problem?

Jeff Good, staff writer for *The St. Petersburg Times,* says, "You've got to make a leap of faith. Ethical decisions are rarely black and white. Sometimes you have to make a judgment call. And you've got to go to bed that night, hoping it's the right one" ("Doing Ethics in Journalism," 1995).

Good Reporting Requires
Organization and Time Management

The news gathering process requires a plan and careful organization of research and ideas. It is easy to get lost in the mass of notes, documents and tapes generated. Following are some basic tips that should help you keep on track so you are ready to start writing.

Organizing Your Information

1. Start a simple alphabetical card file of interviewees with names, addresses and phone numbers. This way you don't have to search through scraps of paper to find them. Put key words for identification on each interviewee card, such as "teen mother's godmother, referred by maternal cousin (by name)."

2. Start an audiotape file of interviewees. Label the tapes by name, date and city. Number them to a correlating number on the card in the interviewee card file.

3. Start a folder file of documents. Many times this is done effectively in chronological order. For example: 1984 birth certificate for the teen mother, 1985 baptismal record from the Catholic Church, 1992 county court record filed against teen's mother for child endangerment, 1993 court record of stepfather for sexual molestation, 1997 city police report of teen abandoning her newborn.

4. Develop an action line or "to do" list. This can be done in a table on the computer: Headings could be Task, Contacts (by name/addresses, phones), Completion Date, and Comments, among others. Take advantage of software on most computers that provide personal organization formats.

5. Limit your primary and secondary research by identifying the key issues you are going to cover in the story. If the research is not relevant to those key issues, you can eliminate it.

6. Draft a rough outline of the story and where the parts you've collected fit.

7. With the research organized around your outline, write the story without stopping to looks things up or to edit. Once you have a rough draft, you can do these things and plug in additional information as needed.

8. Include many voices and many sides of an issue in all the steps involved in gathering the news. Ask yourself if you are presenting diverse segments of the population in an honest and fair light.

Managing Your Time

Time management creates much discussion, but few practice its principles. Working for a news agency will require you to meet deadlines, so train yourself to respond professionally at all times. Following are some useful guidelines:

1. Check in and out routinely. It is essential that your editor knows where you are at all times. If your research and interviews take place over a period of time, tell your editor you'll check in by phone each day or every other day. Keep the editor posted on the progress of the story.

2. Keep a datebook and address book combination.

3. Prepare yourself for research: press ID card, pad, pens and pencils, parking change, cellular phone, address book, laptop, extra disks, tape recorder, electric cord, batteries, extra blank tapes, raincoat, hat, umbrella, etc. Write up a check list, laminate it and include it in your tote at all times.

4. Update your action line everyday and check off the completed tasks. Make to-do lists daily and check off what you have accomplished.

5. Mark essential to-do activities with an A; mark the next most important tasks with a B. Try to finish the A's daily and work on some B's.

6. Prepare a list of questions ahead of an interview. The interviewee may lead you in another direction, but you won't waste time trying to think of something to ask.

7. Allow blocks of time for interviewing and for writing. Protect your prime time and cluster your phone calls—out and in—by grouping messages.

8. Take rest and lunch breaks. It is amazing what you can accomplish when you are organized and feel good.

9. Keep appointments with interviewees and be on time.

Developing Sensitivity to Diversity

In addition to giving attention to organization and time management, journalists must develop an inner sensitivity to diversity. Identifying racism comes fairly easy when you encounter blatant racism. You can deal with it in a straightforward way. An example is when someone uses an obviously racist word. The harder type of racism to identify and confront is that which is subtle and hidden by layers of social acceptance. This could be the Vietnamese man who was not hired because of his accent, the Mexican American employee who is overlooked for promotion because of the deep-rooted assumption that "Mexicans are lazy," and the African American employee who is asked not to wear ethnic clothing because "It doesn't look right to the public."

N-WORD WILL STING—IF YOU LET IT

By Clarence Page,
columnist for *The Chicago Tribune*

"Dad, what's a nigger?" I winced when I heard my 8-year-old son ask that question recently. Like many other African American parents, I foresaw that day with a sense of dread. It is the day our child discovered the N-word.

"It's not a nice word," I told him.

"But what does it mean?" he persisted, displaying that dogged Page family persistence.

"You know what bad words are. It is not a nice word to call someone."

Like all experienced parents, I tried to avoid showing any shock, for that would only encourage him to say it again. By refusing to acknowledge how much power the word carried, I hoped to reduce its ability to wound yet another generation of Americans, my son's generation.

That's not always easy. Hardly a year goes by without somebody, somewhere, trying to remove Mark Twain's *Huckleberry Finn* from classes or libraries simply because it contains the N-word, even as it offers one of the most powerfully anti-racist, prohumanity messages any novel ever delivered.

. . . The rap generation sounds intent on defusing the negative power of the N-word by using it to death, and as a byproduct, outraging their elders—a goal young people typically view as its own reward.

With that in mind, I regard the N-word the same way my school-teacher grandmother, "Mother" Carrie Page, told me to treat the word "ain't."

"Yes, it is in the dictionary, she said, but so are 'hell' and 'damn.' Each has its proper use, which is not in polite conversation. Our language is like our appearance. Whether we can afford nice clothes or not," she said, "we should always dress our language in the finest garments, not in rags" (Page, 1997).

Racism is the belief that certain races are superior to others. It grants special status to certain races and leads to separation and violence against specific races. It assumes that some races are less intelligent and of a lower class than the "superior" race. People use subtle racism to keep others in lower paying jobs, to keep people living separately from "good" neighborhoods, and many times to keep people in inferior housing.

Mike Haney, vice president of the National Coalition on Racism in Sports and Media, wore a Ku Klux Klan outfit to the 1995 World Series in Atlanta (October 28, 1995), "to show America what it feels like to be portrayed in a negative manner." Haney was part of a Native American protest against the American Indian symbols used by fans of the Atlanta Braves and the Cleveland Indians (Associated Press Atlanta, 1995).

In March 1995, in Novato, California, an 18-year-old San Marin High School student was a victim of a hate crime. Glenn Chun was accosted when leaving a fast-food restaurant downtown. Several people started calling him names and then knocked him down. He was called "a chink, a gook, a Chinaman." At one point one of the attackers yelled, "Go back to China where you belong," although Chun is a fourth-generation American. He identified several of his attackers as fellow students at the high school where, of the 940 students, 85 percent are white (Mead, 1995).

Journalists need to interview and report with care the circumstances surrounding a story when race is involved. Sometimes they are duped into believing racist groups' propaganda, which misleads the public. For example, some groups disguise their identity behind words such as democratic, patriotic and liberty. The Liberty Lobby based in Washington, D.C, for example, is the largest propaganda organization in the United States promoting anti-Semitism. Its newsletter has 100,000 subscribers. A key theme of this group is that the Holocaust was a "hoax."

Finding Multicultural Resources

David Holley, Beijing Bureau Chief for the *Los Angeles Times*, says that in most ethnic coverage it is appropriate to report largely through the perspective of community members. Holly has learned to speak Japanese and Mandarin Chinese. He says he immerses himself in research, maps out his approach and keeps an open mind when approaching a new story.

He says in covering a story about the growth of Koreatown in Los Angeles, his first priority was to talk with Korean Americans who gave him the history of that community and the dynamics of its growth. He says he usually looks for a clear, general understanding of an issue, as well as specific anecdotes for illustration.

Holly says he window-shops in ethnic communities and attends festivals and cultural performances. He reads bilingual newspapers and suggests reporters sign up for a foreign language class, which gives an understanding of what an immigrant goes through when entering a country where another language is spoken (Asian American Journalists Association, 1991).

Reporters and photographers would do well to know the demographics of ethnic groups within their news agency's geographical range. What's the population, how many businesses, enrollment numbers in schools, numbers using social services, customs and holidays? For example, if you were writing about the Vietnamese, consider the following profile.

A CULTURAL PROFILE

Cultural Considerations
When Interviewing Vietnamese

1. Vietnamese sometimes laugh or smile to show embarrassment. They may cover their mouths.

2. The given name comes after the family name. Ngoc Lam: Ngoc is the family name, but he is called Lam. Nguyen is a family name used by about 50 percent of the population. Women keep their own family name, but children are named after the father's family. They maintain strong family bonds.

3. Actions are communicated gently. Don't shake hands unless they offer.

4. On leaving, say something nice: "Best wishes to your family" or "Good luck to you."

5. Vietnamese nod their heads vertically to mean they HEAR you; they may not be agreeing with you. Direct eye contact is avoided, especially by females. It is rude to point your finger at someone.

(continued)

A CULTURAL PROFILE (continued)

6. The Vietnamese people revere courtesy, the aging and those in authority.

7. This culture has a strong need to preserve social harmony, which makes them prefer consensus to individual decision making.

8. Marriage and children are expected. Large families are good. They are a pension for old age. Sons are preferred. The daughter goes to her husband's family when she marries. Having a baby out of wedlock is socially unacceptable. There is family rejection and losing face.

9. Education is held in high regard.

10. There are 54 different ethnic groups recognized in the country of Vietnam (Ellis, 1995).

From *Culture Shock! A Guide to Customs and Etiquette, Vietnam* by Claire Ellis, Graphic Arts Center Publishing Company, Portland, Ore., 1995. Used by permission.

WORKING THE BEAT

Exercises

1. Clip a news article about a person. What does the story say about the person?

Does the article include address, occupation, age, gender, race, religion, ethnic group, physical ability, language, political affiliation, community group affiliation, personal background or professional background? Where this information is provided in the story, do you think it's relevant to the story? If you were an editor and could only include five of those facts, which would you choose and why should readers know this? How would it help them understand what is happening in the story? (*Newsday*, 1997).

2. As a special assignment start a diversity interviewee file. Include at least 25 names, addresses and phone numbers and the reason (topic) you would interview them.

3. Develop an enterprise story focused on one of the diversity groups above. Discuss what you did to make it accurate, balanced and complete.

(continued)

WORKING THE BEAT (continued)

---

4. Break the class into small groups. Each group should do this exercise and bring the results together with a class compilation to be used for discussion.

Exercise: Draw the first image that comes to mind when you think of
> a white woman cleaning house
> an Asian American man reconciling his accounts
> a black woman cooking
> an Hispanic man driving a truck
> a Native American man with a glass in his hand

4 Interviewing With Awareness

———————◆———————

Interviewing is considered primary research for an article. Reporters talk to the source or sources for direct information about the details of the story. It may seem that talking with someone would be an easy part of the total article formation, but interviewing skills are varied and need particular attention in order to collect the facts needed for the finished article.

Be aware that not every piece of information you get from an interviewee is reliable. People under stress and for self-protection will give you their perceptions, which may or may not be accurate. Double-check all interview information. Certainly, opinions are valid, and you can use some of these in the article, but the most reliable are facts you can check for accuracy.

———————◆———————

Preparation

1. Researching the Article Background

Approach each story, having done background research. This is not as easy for a broadcast reporter as it is for a print reporter, but it should be done. Even a quick on-air interview can be prefaced with several

---

CHECKLIST FOR INTERVIEWS

Preparation

1. Researching the Article Background
2. Setting Up the Interview
3. Face-to-Face Versus the Telephone Interview
4. Planning

Conducting the Interview

5. Dressing Appropriately
6. Establishing Rapport
7. Taping Versus Note Taking
8. Observing and Active Listening
9. Controlling the Interview
10. Closing the Interview

---

phone calls so you don't sound uninformed about the subject. Busy people hate being asked dumb questions, and it definitely is a dumb question if the newspaper ran the answer this morning.

Sometimes the print reporter has time to do more in-depth research. Libraries and databases are there for the reporter so accuracy and balance are included in the article.

2. Setting Up the Interview

Call ahead and allow plenty of time for the interview. Sometimes a telephone call is all that is needed to get a 30-minute interview the day after tomorrow. At other times, interviewees may want a written outline of your story ideas and/or questions you will ask at the interview so they can prepare.

Follow the interviewees' leads so they can be as comfortable and as prepared as possible. Aim for at least an hour interview. This will give plenty of time to avoid rushing and time for a relaxed interchange to take place.

If interviewees are coming to the city, it's a good idea to write them first, outlining the article and explaining why you want to interview them for this story. Tell them in the letter you will telephone them within a week to confirm.

3. Face-to-Face Interviews Versus the Telephone Interview

Types of interviews vary, such as face-to-face and telephone. Even letters can be a type of interview. The purpose of the interview is to get people's perception of the facts and their observations. You will use the material to get quotations and anecdotes for the article.

The telephone interview is handled somewhat differently from a face-to-face interview. All the principles are the same, but the telephone interview will probably be shorter. You may use a tape recorder, but tell the interviewee he or she is being taped. Because you are missing the visual, you must pay close attention to the words and the emphasis placed on the words when talking on the telephone. Remember, though, that certain cultures may not be comfortable using the phone.

The face-to-face interview is the most reliable. Not only do you get the words from the interviewee, you get to observe the nonverbal language. You should be familiar with American body language as well as with that of each cultural group in your community. The body language of various cultural groups can be noticeably different from the body language of others who have lived in the United States for a long time.

For example, Asian women and children are taught it is disrespectful to gaze directly into the eyes of the person to whom they are talking. If you interpreted this through American body language, someone who doesn't look you directly in the eyes may be lying or hiding something. Be aware of the differences.

The article also takes on added dimension when body movement is described. What do the interviewee's gestures mean, the eye contact, the facial expressions and the use of personal space? The reporter should observe tactile communication: the handshake and use of touching, such as hugging or pats on the back.

The interview will be influenced by the day of the week, the time of the day, the location of the interview such as an office or restaurant, and the positioning of the furniture when you do the interview. This influences the quality of the interview.

Comfort of the interviewee is first. Speak up if some element interferes with the interview, such as having an interview by a street where the traffic noises will drown out the voices on the tape recorder.

Other nonverbal communication affects the interview, and the reporter must always be aware of setting the atmosphere so the reader can participate in the story. Four broad categories of nonverbal communication that should be considered in the story are these:

- *Physical*—facial expressions, tone of voice, sense of touch, sense of smell and body motions.
- *Aesthetic*—creative expression such as playing instrumental music, dancing, painting, singing and sculpturing.
- *Signs*—mechanical communication through signal flags, an alarm clock going off, a factory whistle or sirens.
- *Symbolic*—communication through religious, status and ego-building, such as a Catholics crossing themselves or someone entering a limousine (Acker, 1992).

4. Planning

In your own mind you should *define the purpose* of the interview. Purposes differ, depending on the story. If you are interviewing the newsmakers, you want to know what it felt like to be inside the skin of the people involved. You want their first-person stories. You want the chronological facts as they experienced them. If you are interviewing experts about the trauma involved by having experienced the event, you are seeking psychological information about the impact on a person. These experts were not at the event, may have never met the newsmaker, yet can provide valuable information for your story because of their expertise in human behavior.

Go into each interview with a set of planned questions. Approximately 10 questions are appropriate for one hour. This list will serve as your framework, but it is not set in concrete. The interviewee will come up with information you didn't have, and it is probably more valuable to let them take the lead after you have introduced the topic.

If you are a broadcast reporter, you have equipment considerations, time-of-day considerations, and of course, deadlines to meet. Additionally, you must think of your own appearance, the types of questions you will ask, and a mental walk-through of the interview. You also have to work in your background research.

Print journalists must do their background research, think through and prepare equipment, like the tape recorder or camera, and make other physical considerations involved in the interview. Time must be spent working on the interview questions and designing them to get the information needed for the story.

Conducting the Interview

5. Dressing Appropriately

Having to think about clothing is a bother, but it is part of nonverbal communication you are giving the interviewee. If you are neat, clean and dressed in business clothes, the interviewee will more likely feel you are credible and trustworthy. Dress as nearly like the interviewee's setting as possible. For example, if you are going downtown to an office for the interview, a business suit, sports coat and slacks or business dress is appropriate. If you're interviewing at a picnic, dress casually.

Sometimes radio reporters and behind-the-scenes television writers are the most casual. Don't forget you're on stage too and just because the viewer can't see you, the interviewee and his or her colleagues can. On-air television reporters know that they're shown along with the story so usually they are more aware of what to wear.

6. Establishing Rapport

When you meet the interviewee, you should use all your communication skills to make the interview a success. Greet your interviewee properly and set the stage for a comfortable conversation. If you are recording, set up the tape immediately and test it. The camera person should have established the best position from which to record the interview. If you are alone and have to double-up and shoot photographs, do this at the beginning. Then you can relax and concentrate on the person, and what they have to say.

When you first meet someone, it is best to greet the interviewee with light and nonthreatening comments and questions: "What a great office! Have you been here long?" Think of your questions as a spiral of communications. At first you are on the outer rings of the spiral and each ring leads you in to more intimate knowledge of the person and his or her knowledge pertaining to the story. Work your way slowly into the spiral because this makes it nonthreatening to the person.

7. Taping Versus Note Taking

Even when using a recorder, you will probably take notes. When you prepare your questions for the interview, leave spaces after them so you can enter such things as the spelling of a name; "His name was Laerzeph? How do you spell that?" The recorder can't give you this kind of information unless you ask for it.

Note the numbers corresponding on the tape recorder so you have easy reference to a particular topic. For example, you're down at question 4, and you note the recorder is on 123. Write 123 down by the question.

The tape recorder is your insurance for accuracy. Tell the interviewee "I hope you don't mind if I tape record this. It will help me get your quotes exactly right." Most people today do not mind being tape-recorded, but if they do, turn it off and take notes.

Take plenty of extra tapes. As you set up the recorder, put it halfway between you and the interviewee, turn it on high volume, and pretest it to be sure it is recording. Make every effort you can to hold the interview away from distracting noises such as traffic, air conditioners or office machines.

When you transcribe your tape you will find that the speaking pattern of the interviewee is different from the way you would take down the information in writing. This is one great advantage of the tape recorder. The different voices you include in the article will stand out.

NOTE-TAKING TIPS

Be Prepared. Think ahead before the interview and prepare equipment. You may need pencils, pens, reporter's notebook or steno's notebook. If you use a tape recorder, take extra batteries, a 15-foot electrical cord and extra blank cassette tapes. Sit close to the speaker or interviewee. Don't let the mechanics of the tape recorder detract you from careful listening to verbal and nonverbal cues.

Use Shorthand. If you do not know shorthand or speed writing, develop your own symbols so you can quickly jot down ideas during the speech or interview. Following are some examples:

~	approximately	@	at
w/	with	w/o	without
=	the same	ff	following
+	and or also	*	most important

Review Notes. Go over your notes immediately after the speech or interview. At that point the thoughts, ideas, and facts you may not have noted are still fresh in your mind. Fill in the blanks.

After you are a practiced reporter, you can pull out the quotes you need without transcribing the whole tape.

8. Observing and Active Listening

Observation skills are extremely important in the interview. What is the person wearing? What do they do with their hands? What is the sound of their voice like? The best writers use all of the sensory details when observing. Many stories just describe what is seen and what is heard. The pro includes the smells, the touch and the taste of the situation.

Suppose you are interviewing elderly adults in a convalescent home. The story involves abuse and neglect of the patients, and you want to demonstrate this in your article. You can describe what the facility looks like: gray, cheerless walls with torn wallpaper and grease

HOW TO IMPROVE LISTENING SKILLS

1. Prepare to Listen	6. Listen for Main Points
2. Know Your Own Biases	7. Listen for More Than Words
3. Don't Be Distracted	8. Concentrate
4. Be Open-Minded	9. Be Interested
5. Be Empathetic	10. Delay Judgment

spots on the carpet. You can interview patients and use their words to describe what goes on: *Mrs. Chen said, "They don't always come get the dirty dishes after every meal."*

Now you've got the picture, but how about smell, touch and taste? The smell in the hall is of old urine and pine disinfectant. When you run your hand across the top of the television set in the recreation room, you get a thick layer of sticky dust. When you eat in the dining room with your interviewee, you taste the bland, starchy rice, gray burger and the wilted peas. Now you've put the reader into the picture.

Active listening is a term used to describe attention-giving on the side of the listener. The reporter needs to develop skills to help capture the essence of the interview. Active listening encompasses the words of the interviewee, but the nonverbal communication is equally important. The reporter must actively observe and record the mood, the feelings, even the touch and smells of the interviewee.

9. Controlling the Interview

Although textbooks have extensive lists of types of questions to ask, there are two basics to remember about questions. A direct or closed-ended question will give you a short factual answer. You may be able to get some of these answers elsewhere, but sometimes you may need to ask a few, such as "How many children do you have? How long have you lived in this country? How many people did you see on the night of the accident?"

The second type of question is open-ended. It goes much deeper into the communication spiral: "How do you feel about being a father of three children? Do you feel if you had lived in this country longer, you would have understood the laws they say you've broken? What did you think when you felt the impact of the child's body on the hood the night of the accident?"

Use your own written questions as a guide, but allow the interviewee freedom to explore different areas of the story that you may not have thought about.

10. Closing the Interview

When you have finished the interview, turn off the recorder. Pack up your equipment and figuratively leave the door open with your interviewee. Ask if you may call if questions come up later while you are finishing the story. You may not like the person, but keep a professional demeanor so you can always go back for more information. You may have to do a follow-up interview later. Put your personal feelings aside. You may detest the child molester or the murderer, but to get a story from all sides, keep an open mind and listen.

If the interview has been positive and the interviewee has gone out of his or her way to accommodate you, write a note of thanks. This is a basic courtesy and will make you stand out among your peers. People talk in close communities, and you can build a positive, trustworthy reputation. Your peers may wonder how you're able to get in doors they cannot. Be an ethical journalist. When you say you will do something, do it. When you say you will be somewhere at a certain time, be there. Don't betray confidences of the people who are helping you do your job.

Ken Metzler, in his book *Creative Interviewing,* advises beginners to develop self-confidence by doing their homework ahead of the interview. Preparation is the key to confidence.

He also stresses getting complete information by collecting the 5 W's and How. The tape recorder is recommended, but even in note taking, the interviewer can remember to capture the vital 20 percent of the information.

Additionally, Metzler advises the beginner to learn to make people feel at home and to control the run-amok interviewee. He says to be repetitious about the areas you want to explore and tell the interviewee why their information is important to the story. He urges the beginner to listen carefully and probe deeply into important information.

His last advice is to be sensitive to cultural considerations. Simple social rules apply: Don't talk to a child without permission of a parent or guardian. Set up the interview ahead of time; don't just pop in on the person. Know updated terms used for races, for women, for the disabled, for the aging. Calling a person an *Oriental* when it should be *Asian* or *Korean*, calling a woman a *girl*, calling a disabled person *crippled*, or calling an older adult an *old man* is not going to win you any points.

Working With an Interpreter

There may come a time when you have to use an interpreter for the interview. With this in mind, several considerations should be made. First, the purpose for using the interpreter is a verbal translation; therefore, you need someone who is fluent in the language. There are several problems you must consider. If you use someone unknown to the interviewees, they may not be as comfortable as with someone they know. Just be aware that when using an interpreter, intimacy may be risked. Using a friend or family member of the interviewee as an interpreter may make the interviewee more comfortable, but the down side of this is that if there is something to hide, the interpreter may not give you all the answers or may change them to protect the individual or the community.

When using an interpreter, arrange the setting where all involved can face each other. Do not speak more loudly than usual. Sometimes people think the louder you say it, the better the person can understand. Be patient with slow answers and be ready to reword your questions several ways.

Jade Moon, news anchor for KGMB-TV (Channel 9) in Honolulu, describes her problems in Hawaii where many languages are used. Moon is Korean and Japanese, but she is not fluent in Japanese. She says she remembers an incident when a famous Japanese movie star was arrested at Honolulu International Airport for having drugs in his undershorts. Moon said she had to interview visiting Japanese tourists as well as officials for the story. To the Japanese, privacy is important and aggressiveness is discouraged, especially from a woman.

Moon's photographer happened to be fluent in Japanese, and he acted as the interpreter in this case. She said she asked something like "How do you feel about this famous hero being caught with drugs in his underpants?"

The interpreter had to socially tone down her question to "How does this feel to you that such a man of stature is caught in this compromising situation?"(Moon, 1996).

There are other forms of interpretation than second-language interpretation. If you are interviewing a hearing-impaired person, he or she may have an interpreter. You should be directly facing the hearing-impaired interviewee so he or she can see your facial expressions and read your lips. The interpreter should be beside you facing the interviewee so he or she can read the sign language and sign. The hearing-impaired person has to look back and forth between the two of you, so speak more slowly than you ordinarily do so the person has time to take in the information.

Establishing rapport with sources is important and essential to further contacts. Murray Dubin, the *Philadelphia Inquirer*'s first ethnic beat reporter, says he always ends an interview with "Is there anyone who is even smarter than you? They laugh and give me two names" (Rich, 1994).

Another good ending question is "Is there anything else you'd like to discuss about the topic?"

WORKING THE BEAT

Exercises

1. Research the background of a diversity topic and interviewees you will write about for a class assignment. Organize a system that includes all your research (primary and secondary) in preparation for writing the article. Share this organization system with the class.

2. Prepare a list of 10 interview questions you are taking to an interview related to the above class assignment.

3. Transcribe an entire audiotape of an interview word-for-word. Highlight on the transcript the quotations and the anecdotes you will use in the article assignment.

4. After an interview, describe in writing the setting of the interview using all five of the sensory details. Also include in this paper a description of the nonverbal elements you observed in the interview.

5. List five diverse groups within your community reporting range. List five stereotypes for each of the five groups. Discuss how you can avoid these stereotypes in reporting.

5 Writing and Editing the Diversity Story

◆

Writers say the most difficult part of the writing process is getting started. Once you have interviewed and done the research, you design the story around these facts. How do you begin?

Identifying Story Topic, Purpose and Reader

You should be able to state the **topic** of the story in one sentence. It is much like the nut graph or angle. It is the point of the story: *City budget cuts have forced the administration to limit police officers to one per vehicle on the early morning shift.*

The **purpose** of the story is why you are writing it. Obviously, from the above information, the purpose of this story is to tell citizens that there will not be as many police officers available and on call in the early morning hours in the city. State the purpose in one sentence.

A last consideration is to **empathize with the readers or viewers.** What are their special needs and interests in the story? They would probably want to know: How many fewer police will there be? How long will the response time be now? Is there any way citizens can protest this cut to City Hall? Has this happened in other cities? Has the crime rate

in those cities increased? How can citizens protect themselves against criminals in this time of decreasing police
protection? Have the cuts been made in all neighborhoods
or just in minority neighborhoods?

◆

On the other hand, considering readers' interests does not condone
profit-driven journalism, which Howard Kurtz, press critic for *The
Washington Post*, calls "Pink Flamingo Journalism." He says, "The very
notion that newspapers must study their readers' habits, as if they were
some exotic species, is a stunning sign of desperation, of the missing
synapse that once provided the spark for daily journalism"(Kurtz,
1994).

There is a rush among those who must answer for newspaper
profits to run polls and surveys in an attempt to exactly pin-point the
news their readers want. The danger in this is in omitting total community news.

Developing Skills for
Accuracy, Balance and Clarity

The highest compliment you can receive as a journalist is that you
are a careful reporter, meaning that even with all the time limitations,
you make every effort to check the accuracy of the information through
verification and documentation. First, **accuracy** means checking all the
details.

Welcome your editor's input. As painful as it is to the writer to have
someone question the writing, someone else will catch discrepancies
and errors. If the story involves a minority or special interest group,
check all cultural references and spellings for accuracy with someone
in that community. Just because the newsmaker or witnesses spell
something for you, this doesn't mean it is correct. You should have
sources in the community where you can double-check.

Albert R. Hunt, executive editor for the Washington, D.C., bureau
of *The Wall Street Journal*, talks about his early reporting days at *The*

Philadelphia Bulletin. He says, "One of my first stories was to write an obituary about a woman named Florence Hay who wasn't famous to anybody but her family and friends. My city editor, Earl Selby, passed by as I made some sarcastic remark about this not being on the cutting edge of social change. He pointed out to me there may only be a handful of people who will read that story, but their entire impression of *The Bulletin* will be determined by whether I got it right or not. An error in a date or spelling of a relative's name at a moment of such magnitude would be devastating to them.

Selby thundered, 'You should hate making a mistake.'"

Hunt says, "In more than three decades that was one of the two most profound pieces of advice I ever received" (Hunt, 1995).

A broadcast journalist should check the pronunciation of names: get the spelling accurate, then phonetically spell out the name in parenthesis after the name. Nothing weakens credibility more than some news reporter or anchor stumbling over a person's name, or the misidentification of the name of a cultural holiday, or some cultural icon. For example, Kwaanza is not "African American Christmas."

Kwaanza takes place from December 26 through New Year's Day. It was started in 1966 to instill a sense of racial pride. The holiday honors family, community and culture. Participants are invited to study the seven principles of Kwaanza daily during the holiday and then apply them to their daily lives throughout the year. The seven principles are unity, self-determination, collective work, cooperative economics, purpose, creativity and faith (Baldridge, 1997).

Balance is the second essential element of a news story. Balance means telling all sides of the story. Any time an issue is discussed, both sides should be told. This involves interviews and quotes from all sides. Balance involves fairness too. It is hard to define both, but they involve honesty. Tell the reader the truth from all sides. Leaving out vital information biases a story and leaves it unbalanced and unfair to someone involved.

Clarity is the third element of these important three. Writer Gay Talese said, "I wish somebody had warned me in my youth of how difficult it is to achieve clarity in writing, and to have also added that, with age and experience, it never gets easier" (Writer's Digest, 1995).

If the story is not clear, it is of little value. In order to write clearly, you must comprehend all the details of the story. After that, use simple words, sentences and paragraphs to tell the story logically and clearly. The mechanics of the language you are using should be exercised so skillfully that the reader can read the message without the obstruction of vague words or obtuse sentence constructions. Master the skills, and then tell the story.

Author Rick Bass says, "Show, don't tell. Writing and reading are acts of discovery. 'Telling' robs a story of the feeling of discovery." (Writer's Digest, 1995).

Use the **Authority Techniques**—examples, quotations and numerical concepts—to make your writing strong. These techniques should be used in all your stories to show the reader the story. Take the following elements of the story and look at the weak *telling* and the strong *showing* techniques:

Examples

Telling: *The mother was emotional about the death of her son.*
Showing: *With tears streaming down her face, the mother sobbed when the police officer told her of her son's death.*

Quotations

Telling: *The accused said he was sorry he had to go to prison.*
Showing: *The accused screamed, "My God, I can't stand to think of being locked up for 20 years."*

Numerical Concepts

Telling: *Many teenaged males are killed each year by other teen males.*
Showing: *Last year in this state, police records show that 145 teen males were killed by other teen males.*

Telling a Good Story

Theodore Cheney in his book, *Writing Creative Nonfiction*, says that nonfiction is the literature of fact. He recommends using summary or dramatic leads and many sensory details. Stir up the emotions because they are integral to the thought process. Describe people in groups: how they do what groups do, games they play, fashion and food fads, prices they pay for items they can't live without, and bits of conversation. He also says the writer must zero in on the individual's life. What are the details? Describe gestures, clothes, favorite drinks, hobbies, characteristic behavior patterns, dialect, jargon and specialized knowledge (Cheney, 1991).

John Seigenthaler, chairman of The Freedom Forum First Amendment Center, said in a newsroom training conference, "Journalism is history in a hurry; yes, news is history's first draft; but it is so much more than that. And the talent to tell the story is rare in this society. Sometimes it is a natural gift. Sometimes it is an acquired talent. Those who teach and those who coach have such wonderful opportunity to open the minds of young journalists to this role as storyteller" (Seigenthaler, 1995).

The art of storytelling is essential to pumping interest into an article. It can be the most common and mundane story—"Fire Downtown"— but with storytelling techniques, the event comes alive for the readers and makes them care about the people involved and care about the life issues that might eventually affect them.

A straight news story about a hotel fire, for example, presents the essential 5 W's and How of the story: a 60-year-old mid-town hotel burned almost to the ground at 10:30 last evening. The fire was apparently set by a homeless man, falling asleep while smoking in bed in one of the rooms. Now, of course, readers want to know if anyone was killed or injured; yes, this man was killed; 20 other people escaped the fire without injury. Readers want to know: Who owns the building? Was it up-to-standard for fire safety? How much financial loss was there? Will the building be rebuilt, or will the lot be sold for another downtown commercial enterprise?

The Diversity Angle

How does all this relate to diversity? Well, who are the people who live in this hotel? They are all homeless and have been given vouchers by social services. How did this connection take place? How do social services investigate the safety of these hotels they pay? Now you see how the story expands.

The above information creates the details journalists are taught to collect to tell the basic story. Many times, newspapers and television will run the straight news story first and the follow-up with a related news feature. How can you expand the information and tell the story of how this man met his destiny at this particular time and place?

This man was a 55-year-old former dentist from a large city in the south of the state. He at one time had a thriving practice, a wife, three children and supportive extended family and friends. He was an alcoholic who, after decimating his practice and ruining his relationships, eventually walked away from it all and disappeared from his former life.

In the intervening 10 years the man moved to seven cities, living off welfare and church assistance. He continued to be homeless and continued his alcoholic way of life. This is a diversity story of the disenfranchised.

What does the reader want to know now? What caused this man to come to this ending? What do his wife and children say about him? What do the experts at the agencies he'd contacted say about him and alcoholism? What is the story of his life in this, his city of death? How long had he been here? What agencies had he contacted? With whom had he talked? What other questions would the readers want answered when your article reveals the autopsy shows he was HIV positive?

Roy Peter Clark, dean of faculty at Poynter Institute for Media Studies in St. Petersburg, Florida, says when you start a story, you should think of running into your house and shouting, "Hey Mom, guess what?" The answer to that question is the angle of the story.

Using Narrative Writing Puts the Reader into the Story

Writing consists of four types: narrative, descriptive, expository and argumentative. Sometimes journalists get the idea they are only involved in expository—explaining, giving the facts. Yet, from the above "Fire Downtown" example, you can see that narrative and descriptive writing really show readers what happened. The best articles use not only the lean facts but include fiction techniques such as *figures of speech, dialogue* and *character development.*

Narrative writing tells a story. It is chronological or in sequence, yet it can contain flashbacks. It involves people and their actions and interactions. Narrative usually has some element of drama, with suspense, with foreshadowing and with a climax. All of these characteristics can come into play when you design an article.

When writing narrative, you must have enough detail so a reader knows what is happening, yet not so much that the reader gets bored. The detail must be appropriate in quality and quantity while the reader follows the motion of sequence.

Randall Richard, a reporter for *The Providence Journal*, began his December 13, 1992 award-winning article, *"Freed from communism, but bound by the past,"* with

> The curtain separating his bed from the rest of his parents' one-room flat was bone white and thin, a billowing fog in the midnight chill, and Vladimir Ermon could clearly make out the shadows closing in on his father's bear-like silhouette.
>
> The gray men in the long, gray greatcoats had finally come, just as he always knew they would, but in the muted light from the street lamps of Nevsky Prospekt they were even more terrifying than he had imagined (Fry, 1993).

Edna Buchanan, former police beat reporter for the *Miami Herald*, is a superb storyteller and uses narrative and descriptive details to bring the reader into her articles.

Buchanan (1987) says, "Murder gives you a glimpse into lifestyles that would otherwise remain private. If nothing else, the insight demonstrates again and again that strange things are happening in suburbia—I mean the plain old *Twilight Zone* weirdness.

"What *are* they doing out there and *why*?

"The double murder of a Coast Guard lieutenant and his wife, bludgeoned to death in their handsome, well-landscaped home has never been solved. But a bigger mystery to me is why the couple had 81 neglected, dirty, and unkempt poodles caged in the garage of their expensively furnished home.

"Eighty-one" (Buchanan, 1987, p. 10).

Writing coach Donald Hall (1988) says that each of the most common rhetorical patterns answers a question, and these resemble the journalist's six questions:

Example answers, *For instance?*
Classification answers, *What kind is it?*
Division answers, *What are its parts?*
Cause and effect answers, *Why did it happen?*
Process analysis answers, *How does it happen?*
Comparison and contrast answers, *What is it like? What is it unlike?*
Definition answers, *What is it?*

Style is the paint that colors the total story. Style is defined in many ways, such as your written personality. Style can be whether the article is formal or informal. But style as the key element in writing is defined as the texture of the writing, concerned with *diction, imagery* and *syntax*.

Mark Twain once said, "The difference between the right word and the nearly right word is the same as that between lightning and the lightning bug" (Fitzhenry, 1993).

Reflecting Diversity in Word Choice

Diction means simply the writer's choice of words.

Words name objects; they carry the past value that has been placed on that object. They are symbols that stand for beliefs, attitudes and values. Journalists, as users of these tools, have the responsibility for choosing the appropriate words to put readers and viewers at the scene of the story. Words demonstrate accuracy, fairness and objectivity, all icons of the media world. Words also should reflect diversity and represent as clearly as possible a balanced picture of an event.

The authors of *Doing Ethics in Journalism* (Black, Steele and Barney, 1995) discuss this issue: "Diversity is about the makeup of news organizations and about who is making decisions. Diversity is about the way story ideas are developed and who does the reporting. Diversity is about inclusiveness in choosing sources and about giving voice to the voiceless."

If journalists can subscribe to this principle, then it is easier to understand the power that words carry. A word carries symbols; it carries emotion; it carries meaning; and it carries pictures. On the positive side, words can incorporate diverse groups; words can educate us about our differences; and journalists can use this multicultural rich vocabulary to bring news to life for many groups. Writers should avoid words that demean, diminish, stereotype, patronize or abuse others in any way.

Writers and editors don't always know when they are being offensive with words. Any news agency worth its integrity would not call an African American a "nigger." Yet, use of that word created a tremendous outcry of pain and concern when it was used in the February 4, 1994 issue of *The Sacramento Bee* (Renault, 1994).

The editorial page cartoon by Dennis Renault from *The Bee* that Friday showed two Ku Klux Klansmen speaking approvingly of remarks made by Louis Farrakhan, the leader of the Nation of Islam. Farrakhan said in a news conference the day before that words are not racist, that only actions can do that kind of harm. The cartoon sought to show the falsity of Farrakhan's claim. And it did so by using one of the most powerful and hateful words in the vocabulary.

The Bee editorial page editor, Peter Schrag, apologized to readers during the following week and wrote that the cartoon was meant to address the nonsense of Farrakhan's statements.

Even though the intent of *The Bee* appeared to be on the side of exposing bigotry, the usage of that one word created an outcry from the National Association for the Advancement of Colored People and other civil rights groups. Fahizah Alim, columnist for *The Bee* and an African American, hastened to explain to those who thought the cartoon was innocent. She said in her February 7, 1994 column, "What's in a word? The N word?"

> *For most of America a great deal of pain and shame. For a black person to accept the word from a white person is to accept a symbol of powerlessness. . . . When most black folks hear it from a white person, regardless of the context, what they feel is hatred, and they are enraged by it.* (Alim, 1994)

In daily news coverage, when journalists are covering stories about blacks, the best thing to do is to ask what they want to be called—that is, if their color is relevant to the story. The word *mulatto* is now replaced by *mixed*. *African American* is a term many younger blacks prefer. Others prefer *black*. Some prefer being called *people of color*. To call a black Uncle Tom or Aunt Tomasina is to bring up the stereotype of the black who goes along with the white master.

Editors must be especially aware of words and stereotypes. Good editors are the gatekeepers of the language and must be up-to-date on the latest terminology concerning the diverse community.

Time's First Editor

Briton Hadden and Henry Luce, both young Yale graduates and both white men, started *Time* magazine in 1922. Hadden was the editor of the two. As an editor, Hadden was considered ruthless, noisy and creative. He is said to have guided *Time* writers toward a style of journalism that has become standard: the narrative told by telling the stories of the people involved. Hadden created and imposed a *Time* style.

"He banned attributions to anonymous sources and drew the ire of Southern readers by using the 'Mr.' honorific for black men. At a time when Ku Klux Klan activity was peaking, Hadden directed *Time*'s aggressive civil rights coverage, particularly in exposing lynchings . . . Hadden also developed what became the standard magazine fact-checking system" (Harper, 1998).

Solving Pronoun Problems

Sensitivity involves having and using cutting edge knowledge of the diverse community being covered. For example, sexist terminology has changed since the early 1970s when government guidelines revised job titles from *postman* to *mail carrier*, from *policeman* to *police officer*, from *councilman* to *council member*, and so on. It still exists, though, when only the male pronoun is used. Yet, usually a reconstruction of the idea is possible. Rather than saying "An *applicant* should send *his* form in before July 1," write or say "*Applicants* should send *their* forms in before

July 1." Another way to correct this is to put *the* before form or forms, leaving out the personal pronouns.

Writing About Real Women

Women over 18 years of age do not appreciate being called *girls* or *gals*. They usually do not appreciate, especially in the workplace, terms such as *chick, honey, sugar, darling, dear, sweetie* and other flowery endearments. Most appropriate is calling a woman by her name. Physical descriptions also are sexist many times. Women are often described by the color of their hair, by their slimness or fatness or by their perceived "femininity." Typical is using *a woman mathematician* rather than just *a mathematician*.

Correcting Other Writing Problems

Another area of conflict is in the sports world. Ball team names have come under fire, such as the "Braves," and many news agencies are reporting teams by the city name.

People living with disabilities no longer like the term *handicapped*. The history of this word goes back to the days when people with disabilities had to beg for a living. They sat begging on street corners with *cap in hand* to catch coins from passersby.

Latino people, a grouping that incorporates Mexicans, Cubans and others of Latin descent, complain of the words used to describe their races and cultures. Taco Bell has received harsh criticism for its "South of the Border" promotions. Writing words such as the *head honcho* may not be appropriate within a story. A Jewish person can be offended by the expression *being jewed down*. A Welsh person may not appreciate *welshing on a bet*.

Then the question is: What *can* we write? The best guide is to listen to and understand the people about whom you are writing. Never use language that demeans, diminishes or trivializes a person or group. It is true that media are not always going to get it right, but some basic

THE SAN FRANCISCO
KRON-TV MULTICULTURAL POLICY

The San Francisco KRON-TV Multicultural Policy (1998)
includes the following guidelines for writing and reporting:

◆ Ask your subject what he or she wants to be called.
◆ Avoid references to race in a story unless it is relevant.
◆ Avoid inflammatory language.
◆ Avoid stereotypes.
◆ Avoid double standards.
◆ Use care when using the term "minority."
◆ Be thoughtful and considerate of people's differences.

From KRON-TV NewsCenter 4, San Francisco, 1998.

guidelines help. Words are powerful. Also ask who will be hurt, and who will be helped?

Imagery is another aspect of a writer's style. Print journalists struggle with just the right words that create a word picture for the readers. Broadcast journalists can choose the picture and choose the exact words that complement the image.

Imagery brings up emotion, reader and viewer identification, and mood of the story.

An example of imagery is "The man said he halted outside the chainlink fence because he heard *a junkyard dog* barking."

Syntax describes the sentence construction and how it communicates the message. For example, Ernest Hemingway is noted for his short, simple sentences that create a staccato effect. The sentences are stark and factually to the point, yet they create incredible imagery. Syntax involves the complexity of the writing and conveys the attitude of the story.

Look at the simplicity, yet the power of this Hemingway (1935) quote: *Water buffalo and cattle were hauling carts through the mud. There was no end and no beginning. Just carts loaded with everything they owned.*

The old men and women, soaked through, walked along keeping the cattle moving (p. 23).

Hemingway, who began his career as a journalist, said,

> All good books are alike in that they are truer than if they really happened and after you are finished reading one, you feel that it all happened to you. Afterwards, it all belongs to you: the good and the bad, the ecstasy, the remorse and sorrow, the people and the places and how the weather was. If you can get so that you can give that to people, then you are a writer ("Hemingway Quotes," 1997).

The writer's style is as individual as fingerprints; therefore, word choice and sentence patterns are parts of style, creating attitude. It is important to remember, though, that the strong story line is most important. A writer's style should never overshadow the story itself.

Observation is the journalist's essential tool. The ability to see, to hear, to smell, to taste and to touch are primary elements in describing to the reader the events the reader needs to see. The more sensory detail you use, the easier it is for the reader to get into the story and participate. Details are the fiber of observation. Effective details are obtained by observing and remembering. The journalist's curiosity must be avid and insatiable. Taking notes is essential to remembering.

The photographer has an advantage over the writer because the photographer can take many shots of the action, the scenes, the people and refer to these to complement the story. In reverse, the journalist can use the photographer's prints or tape to remember what happened to complement his or her notes. To observe, you must be aware of your biases and put them aside to achieve freshness.

Avoid news clichés. Don't describe *the crashed car as twisted steel*, show the reader by using fresh ways of seeing—*The car was a mangled collage of tragedy, with four lives forever welded together.*

Setting, or the scene of the events, is crucial to reader understanding. The setting of the event can be defined as the visible background, but in a larger sense, it includes the times and places of the action. The journalist selectively describes the physical setting of a news event by choosing what will back up the *who* and *what* of the story. The time of day can add mood and significance, as well as the social setting of the story. When the journalist writes about four teens killed on Friday night after a dance, the journalist expands the story tremendously when explaining how the dance was a fund-raiser for Friday Night Live, a teen anti-alcohol program. Of course, the driver who ran head-on into the teens' car was drunk. This is the real setting, physical and social.

Viewpoint in article writing can be third-person viewpoint or first-person viewpoint. Usually, straight news stories are written in the third person and features are in both first-person and third-person viewpoint. The definition of viewpoint means from whose mind are the ideas coming. It is the source of the story.

Third-person viewpoint tells the story using third-person pronouns but limits the reader to whatever can be observed by looking at a picture. First-person viewpoint tells the story from the writer's or newsmaker's view as an observer. Which would be more interesting to the reader? Third-person viewpoint, for example, could be from a white, female journalist on reporting at Wounded Knee, or first-person viewpoint from a Native American male reporting at Wounded Knee. For diversity purposes, the white, female view is outside and the Native American view is inside.

Dialogue study is important to the journalist. Quotations are at the heart of a good story, whether in print or broadcast. Generally, the more voices you use, the more interesting the story. A discussion in Chapter 4 about using the tape recorder praises the benefits of writing quotes in the pattern of the interviewee. These different voice patterns stand out against the journalist's and create the benefits of hearing the story from a number of different people.

A journalist may edit quotations to use part of them or to correct grammar, or fill in words that were left out in conversation. The primary rule is not to change the meaning or context of the quotes. Many reporters ask, "Should I write the story with an accent?" Most experts agree that using the word order and word choice of the quotes is important, but the quotations should not be used to demean the person who is being quoted.

An Asian Indian might say, "To ease situation, we sit in living room," whereas, a first-language American might say, "We'll sit in the living room, so we'll feel more comfortable."

Using grammatical mistakes or even slang expressions is acceptable in quotes. You can create characterization of individuals by using their words. For example, The mother of the killer said, *Jimmy never would hurt that baby 'cause he always took good care of his brothers and sisters.*

Jimmy, the killer, said, *I grabbed the baby by the heels and bashed his head against the wall.* See how their language tells the story from two viewpoints.

It is never all right, however, to make fun of people by using a term such as *Jes* for *Yes.*

Characterization directly relates to dialogue, but it is more inclusive. Storytelling involves presenting whole people with whom others can identify. You can show a person essentially in three ways: by the way you write your observations; by using the person's words, their quotations; and by showing them in dialogue with others or using others' quotations about that person.

It is quite common for the journalist in third-person viewpoint to describe the individual: *"The aging man on his knees slumped over the child's body."*

The second way to present this newsmaker is to introduce his words: *"I'd give anything in the world if I could have stopped the car in time."*

The last way is to show him in dialogue with others: The driver of the car, 76-year-old John White of Alexander, sobbed, *"I've killed her! I've killed her."*

The police officer at the scene said, *"There're no way he could have stopped in time."*

Additionally, what do others say about this man? His wife: *"John is an extremely careful driver."*

The DMV official who tested and passed him last Tuesday: *"I don't find many people of his age who have the response time he does."*

The father of the child: *"She turned loose my hand and just darted in front of his car."*

Now you can get the tragic picture of what happened from these words.

You almost don't need any narrative.

Coherence unifies people, places, experiences and ideas in the article. It is the glue that holds the story together. Repeating certain words continues a thought. And particularly, transitional words and phrases create coherence.

If you use *as a result,* you are expressing cause and effect. If you use *meanwhile,* you are showing the reader the time sequence of events.

Likewise, words such as *furthermore* shows relationship of thoughts, *on the contrary* shows contrast of ideas, *likewise* shows a comparison of ideas and *in summary* tells the reader you are ending. These techniques create coherence and take the readers through the mind of the writer.

The *climax* is the turning point of the story when the crucial question or conflict in the story is presented directly, to be solved one way or another. The climax can occur at any place in the story. The inverted pyramid format places the climax at the beginning with the *who* and *what* right away.

Note this quote from Edna Buchannan (1987): *"Gary Robinson died hungry. He wanted fried chicken, the three-piece box for $2.19. Drunk, loud, and obnoxious, he pushed ahead of seven customers in line at a fast-food chicken outlet."*

The story continues with the counter girl telling him his behavior was impolite and trying to calm him. He punches her and the security guard shoots him. The description works because the reader feels the absurdity of a death resulting from impatience caused by alcohol.

Using Interview Materials

As you have seen from many examples, your reader or viewer is not interested so much in your telling what others say but in actually **seeing** and **hearing** what they say. It is not necessary to transcribe each word of an audiotape to capture the 20 percent vital information you need. Listen to the tape and take down the essential quotes, getting ready to plug them into the story. Remember that the good journalist collects much more information than is needed. Don't feel compelled to use everything. Sometimes because of space limitations, you will have to leave out some good material. On the other hand, your stories will be so much more complex and thorough if you have collected a rich background. This will show throughout the article.

Attribution or *credits* are another must for writers and photographers. Everything, every piece of information, every photo or graphic must be attributed. The reader or viewer must clearly know the source of these ideas. Some sources will give you only background information, but others will give you direct quotes and visuals, which are vital to the whole story package.

Rene J. Cappon (1984), author of *The Word*, says quotes perform certain standard functions for writing:

◆ To document and support third-person statements in the lead and elsewhere.

◆ To set off controversial material, where precise wording can be an issue, as in legal contexts.

◆ To catch distinctions and nuances in important passages of speeches and convey some of the flavor of the speaker's language.

◆ To highlight exchanges and testimony in trials, hearings, meetings and other garrulous encounters.

Choosing a Story Format

Formats are naturally changing now from the *inverted pyramid* in the electronic age because it is possible to know exactly how much space is needed for a story. The inverted pyramid originated so editors could cut off the endings of stories when they ran out of space.

1. The *inverted pyramid pattern* is what it says. At the wide top of the pyramid, you include the *5 W's and How* in a summary lead. The nut graph, the main focus or point of the story, comes next. Then you pick up each detail in descending importance.

Inverted Pyramid Pattern Example:

Summary Lead—"A five-alarm fire destroyed 20 acres of brush in South Highlands Tuesday afternoon and left two firefighters injured. Winds of 40 miles per hour caused the fire to shift toward the east, engulfing firefighters in the smoke. The two injured firefighters were treated on-site for smoke inhalation."

Body—Develop the most important points in declining order.

End—Least important point.

2. The *hourglass pattern* is more like the old feature pattern because it has an ending. The article starts by giving the most important

hard news facts at the top. It continues with chronological storytelling for the rest of the story. But rather than ending with the least important information at the end as the inverted pyramid, the hourglass ends with an important ending, such as a wrap-up quote.

Hourglass Pattern Example:

Lead—"The Montgomery City Council cut $100,000 from the Arts Coalition budget when the council met Tuesday evening at city hall. The drop in city tax collection will cause this second cut and will decimate the arts programs for the new year, according to the Arts Coalition President John Gates.

Quote by Gates.

Body—Tell the rest of the story chronologically. Develop each point.

End—"Art patrons including those working with the Montgomery Opera Company, the Montgomery City Chorus, the Writer's Workshop and the Montgomery City Symphony each had representatives who spoke before the council to protest the cuts.

Writer's Workshop President Mandy Williams said, "This egregious disregard for culture on the part of the council will cripple the city art programs for years. A community without arts is an uncivilized place for families and for children."

3. The *Wall Street Journal* pattern is more complex than the above two, but it adds interest and featurizes an otherwise dull story, such as a government meeting. It begins with a soft lead, the nut graph, the supporting points, developments, and ends with a kicker, such as an anecdote, a description or a future action.

Wall Street Journal Pattern:

Soft Lead—"Who would have thought the school board would entertain belly dancers at its weekly meeting on Thursday? A bevy of colorfully-costumed dancers gyrated through the front door of the Main Street School auditorium last night while Continuing Education Coordinator George Hernandez paused while appealing to the board to continue community classes.

Nut Graph—"Community class students were on hand in large numbers to support the continuation of classes ranging from auto mechanics to belly dancers to conversational Spanish.

Body—Develop supporting points.

End—"School board president Henry Bodsworth blushed and laughed as one of the belly dancers led him to the line of dancers to teach him the "how-to's" of Egyptian dancing. With hands on hips and rotating to the music, he promised to consider the importance of community education for the school district."

4. The *list pattern* is useful in its analytical approach. It begins with a summary lead, the nut graph, then leads into two or more lists of interest by using a statement and then a listing of the key points. This can be done several times. After this there is a short elaboration on the story and the ending.

List Pattern Example:

Summary Lead—"Greensville City Police met with the Community Law Enforcement Commission on Wednesday evening to outline the action they will take to strengthen law enforcement presence in the city and in the county.

Nut Graph—"The police and the commission have worked together for eight months to devise a plan of action to cut crime within the city.

Statement 1, List Points

Statement 2, List Points

Statement 3, List Points

Elaborate on the Story—"By combining the efforts of the police and concerned citizens, Greenville now has a substantial plan to combat crime, which includes setting up neighborhood police centers, starting a police education program for all schools within the city limits, and hiring six police officers.

End—"Police Chief Mario Vinci expressed his gratitude to Greenville citizens and to the commission. He said, "Citizen support has been tremendous, and our officers feel the goodwill of the community. I am confident the actions we are beginning will reduce the instances of crime in Greenville."

Be aware that there are many patterns for stories, and because of the precision count of computers, you are not limited as in the past when every story had to be written in the Inverted Pyramid so the ending could be cut if needed. The best procedure is to absorb yourself in the details of the story and let the story tell itself. This type of creativity lends versatility to the electronic medium in use today.

Eudora Welty said, "Each story teaches me how to write it, but not the one afterwards" (Lewis, 1980).

Using Verb Power

Verbs are the most important part of speech. Without the verb, nothing is going on. The journalist should show the story through the actions taking place. Use the verb *to be* and its tenses sparingly and go for the action. Even attribution can be livened up without sacrificing objectivity. Try these verbs for *said: stated, related, shared,* or *added.*

Showing the story in action means using the thesaurus. Build your verb vocabulary. Rather than saying "He *pulled* his brother to safety," could you use *hauled* or *dragged?*

Editing is a rigorous chore. After the stress of writing and re-searching, it is far too easy to quit short of quality. Always spend the extra effort to edit and re-edit.

Dorothy Parker said, "I can't write five words but that I change seven" (Charlton, 1986, p. 41).

EDITING WITH STYLE

Thorough editing is essential to a quality story. A good journalist leaves little for the editor to change. Always turn in your best effort to your editor. Following is a powerful editing checklist:

1. Read the story all the way through, correcting any outstanding mistakes.
2. Be sure the 5 W's and How are right up top in the story.
3. Check pattern and format of article and logical development of ideas.
4. Check grammar of each sentence as well as construction and length.
5. Check spelling and word usage.
6. Check punctuation and Associated Press style (or stylebook in use).
7. Check every fact and quotation for accuracy and placement.
8. Read aloud for rhythm and final mistakes.
9. Ask yourself, "Is the story accurate, brief, clear and complete?"

Writing and editing are both critical areas for the journalist. Writing requires a mastery of the language and the ability to accurately, clearly and completely tell the story to the readers. Good editing is essential also because the credibility of story accuracy can easily be doubted if the copy is filled with errors.

WORKING THE BEAT

Exercises

1. Write a narrative article with vital descriptive details, using the following information. You may fill in any details.

> A female employee of Standard Machines, wearing high heel shoes, was walking toward the elevator on the third floor when she tripped as the elevator door opened and fell into the elevator, breaking her arm.
> She cried, "Oh, I think I've broken my arm."
> Frayed carpet at the opening of the elevator caused her to trip. A coworker who saw the accident called building security who contacted an ambulance for the woman. The Standard employee is suing the building owners for $2 million.

2. Using the following story facts and the four story patterns in this chapter, write a 500-word story in two different patterns. Use these story facts and add any essential details:

> The Air Resources Board met today at the Capitol to vote on whether to postpone the date for banning rice field burning in the area. The original date set for the ban was July 1, whereas farmers want the date postponed for two years so further research can be done on how to dispose of the rice cuttings.
> State Senator Mary Lim said, "Those who have respiratory weaknesses like asthma patients or emphasema patients can't wait two years."

3. Cut the exercise 1 story in half. Now, cut the story to 100 words.

(continued)

WORKING THE BEAT (continued)

---

4. With a classroom partner, exchange the two different patterned articles from exercise 2 and edit your partner's articles. First write your edits on the articles, then verbally explain why you made those changes.

5. Choose an article from this week's newspaper and identify the pattern the writer used. Rewrite the article, using a different pattern chosen from one of the four basic patterns discussed in this chapter.

6 Catching the Image Through Photography and Graphics

◆

Photojournalists have a different challenge from text journalists. Words can be written away from the scene of the news, yet the photographer doesn't get a second chance at capturing in time the event that makes the headlines. Much of what a photographer does is being there at the right time. The news photographer must always be in the thick of the event. For example, more than two-thirds of those journalists killed during the Vietnam War were photographers or camera people (Moeller, 1996).

Other problems also plague photographers, such as the accidental death of Princess Diana in Paris, where celebrity-chasing paparazzi were accused of contributing to the cause of the accident. This has cast a terrible image on other media professionals trying to do their work. Great sensitivity is needed to rebuild public confidence.

◆

Making a Commitment to Diversity

Because of the immediacy of images, photographers must be just as sensitive to diversity issues as writers. Kenneth F. Irby, a photojournalist and associate at the Poynter Institute for Media Studies, says, "I was born and raised in the Washington Hill District. It was a black ghetto when I lived there. When I was about 12 years old, I saw a police drug raid on a house two doors down from ours. I was fascinated with the police photographer. I asked my mom if I could do that.

"She said, 'Blacks don't do that kind of work.'"

Irby says that in spite of his mother's discouragement, he was fascinated with the process. He says the next day he ran out to get *The Washington Post* to read about the story and to see the photographs made at the raid. He saw the image of a black man, bent over and handcuffed from behind, being led away by the police.

"This changed my life," he says.

Irby says he set his course toward a career in photojournalism. He says his mother's stereotyping of what blacks could and could not do was hard to overcome.

His early experiences as a young black led him to work against negative images of his race.

"Show good images of diversity," he urges photojournalists. He says he believes media have a responsibility to educate, to influence the community for change and to reflect diversity images as part of the whole community picture.

Seventy percent of the photographs used in journalism, print and broadcast, involve race and gender issues, according to Irby.

Kenneth Irby, who had his future cast while still a preteen, became a photojournalist for *Newsweek* in New York before going to the prestigious Poynter Institute for Media Studies. He advises photojournalists to be personally committed to expand life information to diverse backgrounds.

His best advice to professionals is this: "Communicate with other cultures, go where they are meeting, don't leave the scene too soon, and don't expect your employer to expand your knowledge of diversity. It is your responsibility to make a personal commitment" (Irby, 1995).

Photographers experience many barriers in trying to perform their craft. They are frequently in physical danger because of the nature of their profession. They struggle with the very physical problems of mechanical equipment, which is knocked about, drenched with water or frozen. They run out of film, they have their film confiscated by police or soldiers, or they are jailed for not having the right passes to an event.

Even with these drawbacks, the professionals proceed so the rest of the world can experience the event. Photojournalists' pictures make an enduring difference in how the public sees the world.

Making Ethical Decisions

Kevin Carter, a white South African photojournalist, risked his life to photograph the evils of apartheid and the ravages of black factional violence. When he went to the Sudan, he "snapped the iconographic image of a starving little girl crawling towards a United Nations feeding station while a black-hooded vulture waited patiently behind her" (Moeller, 1996).

Carter said he never knew whether she made it to the feeding station because people were dying at the rate of 20 an hour. His job was to get the story out. He did and won a Pulitzer Prize. Two months after he accepted the award in New York he committed suicide.

He had told a friend, "I'm really, really sorry I didn't pick up the child" (Moeller, 1996).

Other ethical dilemmas facing imagemakers involve the right to privacy of the individual, the hidden camera antics of news and entertainment agencies, and courtroom "entertainment" such as the O.J. Simpson three-ring circus.

A Washington state newspaper ran the photograph of a child's body in the ash-covered bed of a pickup truck after the Mt. St. Helen's volcanic eruption. Did the photographer capture the essence of this disaster, or did he breach the family's right to privacy in this tragedy ("Doing Ethics in Journalism," 1995)?

A November 1992 ABC "Prime Time Live" story exposed the meat department practices of Food Lion Inc., a grocery store chain. Hidden cameras caught images of employees soaking fish in a bleach solution in an attempt to remove offensive odors and covering expired meat with barbecue sauce before repacking and restocking the product (Moeller, 1996). What are the issues connected to the hidden cameras versus the public's right to know about the safety of the food they buy and consume?

Celebrity Images

Television's tendency to rerun images over and over creates ethical questions. Princess Diana's auto crash and funeral tapes were shown repeatedly over two weeks or more. Many complained that the death of Mother Theresa a week after Princess Di's death was not publicized to any extent compared to the princess, although Mother Theresa has spent a whole lifetime devoted to humanitarian service.

Also, would you attempt to number how many times television, over a period of a year, has shown President Bill Clinton hugging then White House intern Monica Lewinsky before and after his admitted inappropriate relationship?

Repetition does affect attitudes.

After the O.J. Simpson trial in Los Angeles, where the minute-by-minute events were televised for the world to see, legal and court gatekeepers have battled with media professionals to ban cameras from courtrooms. Still, courtroom artists have been allowed so that images are still available to the public. Rather than more answers, there seem to be more ethical questions around these issues.

The televised O.J. Simpson trial polarized blacks and whites and many believe eventually affected the outcome of the jurors' decisions. Racial hatred flared and the world watched the images daily in their own home. Should human scandal and disaster become human entertainment?

A Computer Graphics Problem

Another image of Simpson created a classic journalism textbook case: Both *Newsweek* and *Time* ran cover photographs of Simpson's police mugshot, but the two covers conveyed vastly different visual messages. *Time* sent the photo to an artist to convert to an illustration. The artist darkened Simpson's cheeks and generally made the picture look more sinister and destitute than the actual photograph. Although *Time* labeled the cover an illustration, it received much-deserved criticism. *Time* did apologize for the illustration. Computer graphics have created a whole new world of questions and ethical issues (Lester, 1996).

Avoiding Stereotypes and Omission

Photographs and graphics lend themselves to stereotyping. The one-time quick image works because it uses symbols and icons to get the message across to the reader or viewer. Women have been the butt of jokes in pictures and cartoons for decades because the photographer or artist has only limited space and time to get the message over, and societal prejudice guarantees instant recognition of large breasts and emotional outbursts. This unfortunate reality perpetuates the stereotypical images of women: the sobbing victim of tragedy, the supporting mate of some noted male newsmaker, the ditzy aging crone with a dozen cats climbing all over her.

Asian Americans complain of the goggle-eyed, inscrutable Asian image; Native Americans complain of sports team mascots with tomahawk and feathered headdress; Mexican Americans complain of constant images of them in Chevys, standing before the crucifix and wearing a sombrero.

Think of the human message you want to portray and how you will convey it. If a racial or gender message is part of the story, how can it be shown in a different way? Be knowledgeable about diversity stereotypes.

Some have become cynical about the situation.

John Leo (1997) of *U.S. News & World Report* says, "Diversity reporting is similar to ordinary reporting, except that facts are usually avoided and the central message is that life in America is essentially a racial struggle between whites and nonwhites, which the nonwhites or people of color, will win by becoming the majority in the year 2050."

Omission in images is the universal vortex for photographers and graphic artists. They must become proactive instead of taking the lazy, reactive image-making track. As Kenneth Irby says, there must be a commitment to diversity, to showing the total community.

Image Problems With Cartoons

Cartoonists, both those who draw for entertainment and for political satire, need to be sensitive to the changing community. Women have complained for years about Mort Walker's comic strip, "Beetle Bailey." One of its characters, U.S. Army's Gen. Amos Halftrack, has been sexually harassing his beautiful civilian secretary, the buxom Miss Buxley.

Walker argued that Halftrack's behavior demeans foolish old generals rather than women. Still, in light of the 1990s sexual misconduct in several branches of the military and the problems of harassment in the workplace, Walker changed his tune and sent Halftrack to sensitivity training.

After the training, Halftrack apologized to Miss Buxley and her colleague, Pvt. Blips, "It's just that I grew up with certain words and attitudes I thought were OK. I'm sorry" (Nauman, 1997).

On the other side, cartoonists who draw those greedy sheikhs preying on American consumers say there is no national or ethnic bias involved. They say they are "equally unflattering to Jews, Catholics, blacks and politicians of all ages, races and ideological persuasions."

Paul Szep, a cartoonist at *The Boston Globe*, says, "You can't draw a cartoon and draw beautiful people—Irish, Jews or Arabs. Caricature is not a very pleasing art to the people who are being caricatured.

"I can understand why Palestinians and Arabs feel they've been shortchanged in the American press, and they probably have been. They've only recently started to try to improve their image."

Jeff MacNelly, editorial cartoonist for the *Richmond* (Va.) *News Leader,* says Arabs are fair game, just like anybody else. He says the Arabs' distinctive dress gives cartoonists an easy handle. MacNelly says when you draw a bunch of Republicans, it's easier to draw a bunch of elephants. It's symbolic shorthand (McCain, 1980).

A cartoon aimed at welfare reform outraged black leaders. Mike Lukovich, *The Atlanta Constitution*'s Pulitzer Prize-winning political cartoonist, drew the offending cartoon, published in the newspaper in 1995.

The cartoon depicts a white man holding a black baby by his shirt collar and saying, "Either your unskilled, uneducated mothers get a job, or you're dead meat!" In his other hand, the man holds a piece of paper labeled *welfare reform*. The problem was that Luckovich drew a black baby to represent welfare recipients although an equal number of whites depends on government assistance (Hirt, 1995).

The Sacramento Bee's editorial cartoonist, Dennis Renault, who shocked blacks early in 1994 with his drawing of a KKK member saying of Louis Farrakhan, "That nigger makes a lot of sense," was censored from the Walters Art Gallery in Baltimore where the Association of American Editorial Cartoonists met in June of 1995. The exhibit titled "Worth a Thousand Words" ran through January 21, 1996. Several black security guards complained about the cartoon and a *Baltimore Sun* editor decided to pull it ("Cartoon on racism is still controversial," 1995).

Renault ran into trouble again on February 20, 1996, when *The Bee* ran another cartoon that took a shot at the Native American Rumsey Tribe's donation to the Sacramento Symphony. The drawing itself shows a concert stage and the audience. On stage are two singers in front of a large "Bingo, Native American Casino" sign.

The caption read, "As the curtain rises on the second act of the opera, *The Donation*, Native American leader, Ilfonso, is handing a $100,000 check to the president of the local symphony foundation, John Deepockets, assuring him it is an age-old tribal tradition and unconditional, and he sings the haunting aria, *No Quid Pro Quo*. Deepockets steps forward and answers with *The Indian Love Call*, accompanied by a chorus of desperate arts organizations."

Paula Lorenzo, chairwoman of the Rumsey Indian Rancheria in Brooks, California, said it was a cheap shot. She said Renault is totally ignorant of Native American culture and traditions and gift-giving and sharing are ancient tribal traditions. She further complained that such a characterization implies that an Indian tribe's money isn't as good as a contribution from an oil company, an insurance company or a developer. She says it borders on racism (Lorenzo, 1996).

Employment and Image Study

Part of the problem of imaging is the same as it is in any other area of the media: the staffs at media organizations are predominantly white. Mid-1990s surveys found that little more than 10 percent of the professionals in the nation's newsroom were minorities. Simply by hiring more minorities, more women, more gays, more disabled—a cross section of the community—the news agenda would swiftly change perspective (*News Watch*, 1994).

Our neighbors to the north hardly fare better. A newspaper photo analysis of six Canadian newspapers revealed that out of the 2,141 photographs published in the newspapers during one week in 1993, visible minorities were depicted in only 420 images. Of those, 36 percent were pictures of athletes.

Out of the 895 local news stories published in the same six newspapers, only 14 percent mentioned minorities or were about issues that directly affected minorities. This is less than a 20 percent share of the population minorities occupy in the combined population of the cities ("Visualizing the News," 1997).

Ask for Feedback

One third of newspaper photographers interviewed for an American Society of Newspaper Editors (ASNE) report said that feedback on their work is rare. Therefore, it is a good idea to seek feedback at every turn. Ask your editor, ask reporters, ask other photojournalists, and most important, ask diversity group leaders to give you an honest critique occasionally (ASNE, 1988).

Develop assertiveness about your work. Insist on clarity and accuracy from editors and news managers. Gene Roberts, a former *Philadelphia Inquirer* executive editor, says, "If there is one single thing wrong with photography in American newspapers, it is that photo editors are not given enough voice in the handling, the play and the cropping of pictures" (Morris, 1998).

Few still photographs are published or shown without words of explanation. Photography and graphics regularly come with titles, cutlines, headlines and text. Sometimes the connotation of the image is uncertain, and these words exert a great deal of force on interpretation. Change the words and you change the apparent meaning of the image and thereby help determine its social effect (Lester, 1996).

WRITING GOOD CAPTIONS

The Associated Press (1984) put together a list called, "Ten Tests of a Good Caption," outlining the job of a caption, which is to describe and explain the picture to the reader. They advise, "Never write a caption without seeing the picture."

1. Is it complete?
2. Does it identify, fully and clearly?
3. Does it tell when?
4. Does it tell where?
5. Does it tell what's in the picture?
6. Does it have the names spelled correctly, with the proper name on the right person?
7. Is it specific?
8. Is it easy to read?
9. Have as many adjectives as possible been removed?
10. Does it suggest another picture?

From *The Associated Press Stylebook and Libel Manual,* 1984. Reprinted with permission.

The same professional rules that apply to still photography apply to broadcast and to online journalists who work with both words and photographs. Make sure you give and get feedback from editors.

Graphics in the News

A journalism hybrid, information graphics, has entered the field of print and television with tremendous impact. *Newsweek*'s team of designers, researchers and illustrators typically report, design and draw their work in only a few days (or a few hours), usually under the pressure of shifting space and breaking news deadlines.

It is never as easy as they make it look. To assemble a graphic that can be read and digested in a few minutes usually requires hours of discussion, drawing and redrawing. Subject matter complex enough to warrant a cover story has to be boiled down to a page or two or often less ("Visualizing the News," 1997).

Graphics combine words, photos and drawings to illustrate complex events, concepts and trends at a glance. How can you trace the events leading up to a news burst if no photographer was there? How can you show with just words the shock and disappointment on the face of a disabled woman when she realizes the state has cut by 50 percent the budget of the program that supports her?

Photographers, graphic designers and others who provide the news images that flash through our daily lives need diversity sensitivity, just as writers do. The community cannot help but be better served when imagemakers reflect the realities of the whole community.

WORKING THE BEAT

Exercises

1. Clip five newspaper or magazine photographs of different people who could be labeled diversity community. Analyze each photo: How do you know this photo represents this particular group? Is it stereotypical? Is it a positive or a negative image? Why? What other poses or shots could the photographer have used to accompany the story?

2. Divide the class into five groups. Each member of each group will individually develop two guidelines for "Catching Diversity Images." Each group will consolidate its list. In class discussion develop a list of guidelines for photographers.

3. Invite a print photographer and a television camera person to class to discuss as a panel the "how-to's of diversity imaging." What are their conclusions? After the discussion, show them the guidelines for photographers the class has developed and ask them to comment and add or subtract from that list.

4. Go to the library, analyze one week of front page photos for this year for your hometown newspaper and analyze the same week for *The New York Times*. Which newspaper had the most diversity images: women,

WORKING THE BEAT (continued)

minorities, disabled, etc. Tally the numbers in each newspaper. How do these numbers translated to percentages compared to white males on the front page? To expand this assignment, go back 15 years for both your hometown newspaper and *The New York Times*, using the same week of the month. Have the percentages of diversity images improved in 15 years? Discuss the elements that dictate the news agenda as it relates to photography and graphics.

5. Clip five advertisement photos and graphics from a women's magazine and five from a men's magazine (such as *Elle* and *George*). Analyze for contrast and comparison. Are the messages to women any different in the women's magazine than those in the advertisements in the men's magazine? How are women shown? What role do they take in the advertisements? Did you find stereotypes? How could these be improved?

6. Photography magazines are role models for photographers. Analyze two different photography magazines, looking for diversity images. Analyze the editorial photography and the advertising photography. What did you find? What would you change if you were in charge?

7 Shaping Broadcast Decisions

◆

Covering the community in television and radio involves the same principles of news that exist for print journalism. Yet, one of the major differences between television journalism and print is the moving, visual aspect of television. The newspaper and periodical photograph is static and accompanies articles to bring depth to the reader. The television camera brings the story into the lives of the viewers where they can quickly interpret much of the story for themselves. Television becomes larger than life just by the swing of the camera focus.

John Leonard (1997) in his book *Smoke and Mirrors*, says, "If newspapers are what Fritzsche calls a 'Word City,' television is an Image Megalopolis, an Imaginary Capital. This Realm of Signs is every place we've ever been, or thought we were, and every traumatizing trope (a figure of speech) we brought back like a virus" (p. 265).

The television reporter is concerned with the words, the research and the visuals. The reporter, in addition, must incorporate the camera's view of the story. Not only must words be right, the presentation of the words with sounds are extremely powerful, and then what the viewers see brings the story home. Television and radio both allow listeners to hear the actual source, and this immediacy has changed the news forever.

———————————◆———

Writing for the Eye and the Ear

Broadcast writing should be conversational and clear. Viewers actually see the newscaster talking, and both TV and radio bring the sound of the announcer talking directly to "you." Stiff and convoluted copy is too difficult to follow and not the way people talk with each other. The basics of writing are simple words and simple sentences, placing important information at the top and again emphasizing it with a wrap-up. Whereas print writing uses the inverted pyramid or the hourglass format, broadcast copy is written in a circle.

The start of the circle puts the *5 W's and How* right up top, the points are made within the copy, and the circle meets again at the end when the point of the story is summarized. Broadcast writing, whether for television or radio, is written so that viewers or listeners can pick up the story at most any point they tune in. Television brings the uniqueness and the complications of visuals.

Valerie Hyman, director of broadcast journalism at Poynter Institute for Media Studies, says organize your script: "Know the answer to this question, 'What's the point of this story?' Use narration to deliver objective information such as statistics, locations and order of events. Use sound bites and natural sound to deliver subjective information such as "What was it like?" reaction, opinion, analysis and emotions.

She continues, "Always remember that clarity and brevity come from selection, not compression. Concentrate on the material you could not have gotten over the phone. Use active voice verbs: 'The boy found the body'" (Hyman, "Power Reporting," 1996).

Covering the community uses the same guidelines for broadcast as for print, but the addition of visuals brings the added responsibility of avoiding stereotypes and omitting important diversity leaders from the picture.

Because the newscaster is seen, whether this person represents the community is another important aspect of broadcast journalism. The paucity of people of color working in broadcast adds to the lean coverage of all the news outlets.

Problems for Minorities in Mainstream Television

A study from the University of Colorado on Ethnic Culture and Television News analyzed how ethnic communities and television newsrooms interact. The study's focus was on Hispanics. Several themes came out of the study and are worth noting for future journalists.

From the beginning of their careers ethnic journalists are faced with questions around them such as how they got their job, whether they are able to perform, and whether they will be fairly compensated for the work they do. Immediately, someone must decide whether they will be assigned to the "ethnic beat" or be given a broader range of stories to cover.

At times there is conflict with mostly Anglo, male managers over what will be covered, how it will be covered, and whether these disagreements will jeopardize the reporter's career. Mainstream media values are infused with white maleness, which will likely clash with the Hispanic journalist's perspective. Among the Hispanic community, there is concern over the lack of Hispanics represented in media and over the continuing negative stereotypes we see on television (Heider, 1994).

Women Television Stars

One bright star and role model for Hispanics in television news is Giselle Fernandez who has worked for CBS and NBC. She was born in Mexico of a Jewish mother and a Mexican flamenco dancer father. She calls herself the original "Kosher Burrito." She says she developed her passion for journalism when touring as a child through Mexico with her mother, who was researching a doctoral thesis on Mexican folklore.

Fernandez says, "Traveling the world to interview fascinating people and going behind closed doors for access to world leaders has
allowed me a front row seat as history unfolds."

She interviewed Castro in the first English-language interview in
two decades. She has covered Somalia, the Bosnian war, Hurricane
Andrew in Florida, the World Trade Center bombing trial and the
Persian Gulf War, which earned her an Emmy award (NBC, 1997).
Fernandez has now moved to entertainment television in Los Angeles.

Another exceptional television news woman is Jade Moon of Honolulu's KGMB-TV 9. Moon was born in Hawaii but spent her childhood
traveling the world with her military father and family. Her mother is
Korean and her father Japanese. Moon says her knowledge of diversity
comes from her own family, from her travels and from the multicultural
community of Hawaii.

She advises new journalists to immerse themselves in the culture of
those they interview. She talks about her experiences with the Asian
culture and the different approach to reporting she learned. When she
was covering the education beat for the station, she says she couldn't
understand why Caucasian teachers would talk with her but the Asian
teachers would not.

Moon says that even though she is Asian, she is a strong American
female and took her journalism training in assertiveness seriously. She
eventually found that she could not shove a mike in the face of an Asian
and get an interview. She says Asians do not approve of assertiveness
in females, and they treasure privacy (Moon, 1996).

Although women and minorities are making some progress in
television news, they still lag far behind the white male in all areas
before and behind the camera.

Cokie Roberts, ABC news special correspondent, says, "One issue
that we should be worried about is diversity in the newsroom. In 1964,
when I came into the world of work, it was completely legal for an
employer to say to me, 'Well, we don't hire women to do that. Women
don't have authoritative voices.' It matters to young women doing these
jobs, and that there are women who have gone before them. It gives
them inspiration and courage" (Roberts, 1997).

One problem that exists for television journalists who aspire to be
on camera is that they must be telegenic. Journalists complain of being
turned down because they are not what the industry calls "aesthetically

pleasing." Yet, it may be difficult to meet media beauty standards that are rooted in mainstream values. Women with dark hair who find themselves on the television screen many times find it a necessity to lighten their hair with each passing year—not gray or white but blonde.

Broadcast Time Limits

An extremely limiting element in broadcast is the time allowed for the programs. Not only do print journalists have more time to prepare a news story, but they have more space for words to present the story. A reader can go back to the print story and reread it and use it for referral. The broadcast story is usually on only once—prime time—or modified and run again for the 10 or 11 o'clock news. The stress of the one-time shot and the limited time, usually no more than 1-1/2 to 2 minutes for the long story, make television production very intense (Stephens, 1993).

Yet, even with the time restraints, the commercial networks on their weeknight evening newscasts devoted 1,392 minutes to the O.J. Simpson murder trial between January 1 and September 22, 1995. That is as much time as the Bosnian war, the Oklahoma City bombing and the welfare debate got combined.

Television journalist Judy Woodruff says, "Some people are saying that this just reflects what the American public wants. Yet, it was interesting to watch some supposed sophisticates rail against the O.J. fixation one minute and in the next, break into a lengthy discourse on Marcia Clark's (prosecution) wardrobe or the Robert Shapiro–F. Lee Bailey (defense) feud or the real story of Kato Kaelin (guest house occupant at the Simpson house on the night of the murders)" (Woodruff, 1995).

MediaWatch (October 1997) reported that the death of Princess Diana in August 1997 drew 686 network stories and only 113 stories about the fund-raising investigation implicating President Clinton and Vice President Gore, the two most powerful men in the world. Critics also complain about celebrity death coverage, which they call "Genuflect Journalism."

TOWARD ENTERPRISE REPORTING

by Valerie Hyman

1. Get more voices of those who are rarely on television and more subjects that are rarely covered. Pay special attention to the most vulnerable and the powerless.
2. Go where the pack isn't.
3. Ask different questions when you make your old beat calls.
4. Consider what led to your strongest reaction and recapture that experience in the story.
5. Seek ideas from everyone in the newsroom and everyone in your life.
6. Go to where the puck is going to be.
7. Get the target of your story to open up and tell her/his side.
8. Ask yourself, "Who has the money and the power in this town? Who doesn't?"
9. Turn to your photographer at the end of interviews and ask if she/he has any questions.
10. Figure out which people are closest to the story—the ones whose lives are directly affected by it—and interview them on camera.
    Save officials and experts and spokespeople for the phone and build information you get from them into leads, tracks, and tags (Hyman, "Towards Enterprise Reporting," 1996).

From Poynter Institute for Media Studies, Online, Internet, March 1996. Reprinted with permission.

Little more than a decade ago the three major commercial networks dominated the field, but now with cable there are alternatives and thereby competition. There is increasing pressure to retain public attention for advertising reasons, and it does seem that almost anything goes to grab the attention of those channel surfers. Pandering to public desires may merely reflect the marketplace, but it often debases the journalistic values on which the Fourth Estate is founded.

News Director Daniel Webster of WTVT-TV says, "We've become very good at responding to breaking news. What we're not good at is drawing back and saying, 'Are we asking the right questions?'" (Webster, 1995).

Christine Craft, television and radio personality turned attorney, says people are leaving television news. "In the '70s and '80s, television news was a hot medium; now it is icy cold. The dumbing down of television news in order to appeal to the lowest common denominator and the theoretical largest possible audience has, ironically, left many viewers with few reasons to watch" (Craft, 1996).

Diversity reporting and coverage is going to become an economic factor in the future. Minorities ask for more positive stories and images of their groups. A good, positive example is Tiger Woods, a professional golfer since his junior year in college. Woods' father is half black, one quarter Native American and one quarter Chinese. His mother is half Thai, one quarter Chinese and one quarter white. Woods has become a young role model for the nation. Some say his story is redefining race and who America is.

After winning the top amateur golfing awards, he entered the PGA Tour. He says he has not escaped the bias that minorities suffer and has received threats since he was 16. "That's just the way life is when you're playing a sport that traditionally hasn't been a minority sport" ("Is Tiger Woods Redefining Race, Too?," 1997).

Writing for the Ear

A radio or television station that claims to bring you "all the news" is, of course, a misrepresentation. Broadcast reporters must write a lean story and hope that interested viewers or listeners will pick up the newspaper to get the details. Again, the vital 20 percent of the information is what's important to broadcast.

In a 20-second broadcast all you have time for is *Who, What, Where, When*—and often the *Why* and *How* suffer.

You have to eliminate the historical background except for those few facts that make the latest development significant. Mostly, you eliminate direct quotes because all you'll have time for is quick paraphrasing. The camera shots or sound bytes will pick up quotes from interviewees to enhance the story (Cohler, 1994).

Voice is important on radio and television and the ethnic accent is not embraced. In fact, the only foreign accent that appears to be valued on American broadcast is the British or Australian accent.

Developing a Visual Attitude

All over the United States, television news stories are formatted in blocks running from 30 to 60 minutes. This is true on all levels of all markets, large and small localities and networks or cable. Stories from staff reporters and other sources are rewritten and repackaged for each 60-minute block (Cohler, 1990).

The initial shot of the TV anchor, then the switch to another anchor, to a field reporter and field shots all have to be considered when planning for TV news. Writing to those shots and to graphics requires a visual attitude.

Sometimes a vital news story of the day may be bumped from the top of the hours so a less serious story with a powerful visual can lead in the hour. Then the more important story can come immediately after with more time to explain the developments.

For example, a news agency might lead with a graphic fire story in the city with dramatic footage of firefighters rescuing two children. This story would perhaps affect thousands of viewers, yet a United States Supreme Court's landmark decision on civil rights, affecting millions of people, might be put in second place in the news lineup because the only footage they have is of some of the justices in robes sitting around talking.

Developing a visual attitude is essential in television reporting and of course in videotaping. This distinctive element of TV opens the door to more diversity awareness. Just being aware of the racial, ethnic and gender differences in stories aids in choosing pictures. Be particularly cautious not to show minorities always in negative stories. When have you seen a black, woman physicist being interviewed? How often do you see a person in a wheelchair discussing the ups and downs of the stock market? These people exist and are part of the diverse community that should be covered.

Case Studies of
Diversity Television

Newspapers are now moving into niche journalism where special interests of the customers are being sought and highlighted. It is no different with television. Cable has brought a new era of very specialized programming with foreign language programs and a growing focus on the diversity community.

Kaleidoscope, America's Disability Cable Channel, is directed at the 49 million Americans with life-limiting impairments. Each program features people with a disability and incorporates a variety of services, including open captioning and audio-descriptive narration.

Included in the various programs, Kaleidoscope shows world-class athletes with disabilities, and a show titled "Ablefit" demonstrates a workout for people with disabilities led by people with disabilities ("Diversity Channel," 1995).

Mark N. Trahant, writing for New America News Service, says Native Alaskans, frustrated by the alien world they saw on television, spearheaded a cable show called "Heartbeat Alaska," where Native Alaskans could talk about issues that affect their lives and livelihood. Their chief concern is trying to protect their traditional way of life, which involves hunting and fishing for subsistence.

Whereas Native Alaskans make up some 17 percent of the population of Alaska, they are virtually invisible on television. There are few native reporters in the state in any medium, and this lack of diversity is true of city police departments, university faculty and just about every element of the state's business and political structure. Alaska's first people are defined by others as corporate leaders (there are 13 regional native corporations), drunks or people clinging to a tradition that is no longer feasible.

Jeanie Greene, an Inupiat, went to an Alaskan television station with the idea of airing the native voice. The concept was simple: Let the people in the communities send in their own stories on videotape. At first she was dismissed, but she kept demonstrating her videos until an independent production aired on an Anchorage TV station to more than 250 villages across the state via the Rural Alaska Television Network. Thus, the birth of "Heartbeat Alaska."

A RADIO DIVERSITY CASE STUDY

Lydia Bragger was on the air in New York City at WBAI when the staff burst into her studio with a cake and singing "Happy Birthday." Lydia just told her listeners, "You're at a birthday party."

Bragger was celebrating her 90th birthday at work on the "Gray Panther Report," a program she has hosted since the mid-1970s. She is the self-proclaimed "Oldest Radio Talk Show Host in America." She cofounded Media Watch, which eventually persuaded the National Association of Broadcasters Code Board to add the word "age" to a code book already urging sensitivity in programming with regard to race, color, creed and religion. She complained so much to advertisers about their stereotypes that *The New York Times* labeled her the "scourge of Madison Avenue."

Respect for a senior's thoughts is essential to intergenerational communication, according to Bragger. She says, "There are not enough older people speaking out for older people. There are younger people trying to tell them what they should do. But to address certain issues, you need somebody who has lived" ("Choice Champions," 1994/1995).

From *New Choices,* Dec. 1994/Jan. 1995.

Before the program, Greene says life reflected on television was nothing like that of the people living in rural Alaska. "Now, to see yourself on TV is an amazing thing" (Trahant, 1995).

Examining Radio Differences

In radio the announcer must transport all information through words, sound effects and music. There are no camera lenses to convey a flood's devastation. The announcer, within set seconds and minutes, must present the news story graphically. Although most people get their news through television, millions hear the news through radio first, during their morning commute time to work and their afternoon drive time home. The television news in the evening may expand on the story, but the audience often hears it first on radio.

When television came to the public, a quarter century of radio "watching and listening" was forgotten. Many professionals fled radio for the television stage. A period of time existed when radio became "canned" and suffered from this abandonment. Today, radio offers advantages that TV doesn't, and you can probably name as many radio personalities as you can television personalities.

In smaller markets, radio announcers "rip and read" the news from the morning newspaper or newswires. There is little money for reporters to go out and cover meetings or news events. Many programs are automated, yet live talk show hosts fill up the day with drivel and depth (Orlik, 1994).

A major drawback of radio is the talk show host who discusses news events and issues, leaving the listeners with the impression that whatever is said is a news fact. These are entertainment shows and just that, filled with the host's opinions and those of the listeners who call in. On the other hand, they can be a valued forum for the overlooked diverse community.

Hate Speech on Radio

Most political talk show hosts on the air today are conservative in their opinions on social issues. This generally means minorities, women, ethnic groups, gays and the disabled are either ignored or blasted on the programs.

Hate speech is not a new phenomenon. Radio priest Charles Coughlin is called the Father of Hate Radio. Coughlin was a Roman Catholic priest whose Depression-era (1930s) radio show promoted right-wing populist and anti-Semitic ideas. More than 16 million Americans listened to his "Golden Hour of the Shrine of the Little Flower" (Mann, 1997).

Hate radio is meant to be offensive to special groups. Small radio market talk show hosts have copied the "big guys" who have large markets such as Los Angeles and New York and national syndication shows.

The media send a mixed message to the public about their airing of hate speech on "shock radio." For example, censorship codes that don't allow offensiveness have been used throughout the years to censor political figures and community activists, yet they don't seem to apply to media's own employees.

Large radio markets in New York and Los Angeles promote outrageous talk show hosts such as Bob Grant, Jay Diamond, Howard Stern and Rush Limbaugh. Whatever they air appears to be accepted without censorship. The law protects opinion, and hate radio has taken advantage of this.

Bob Grant–New York WABC, says, "Minorities are the Big Apple's majority. You don't need the papers to tell you that. Walk around and you know it. . . . To me, that's a bad thing. I'm a white person" ("Single standard on bigotry needed," 1994).

Jay Diamond–New York WABC, like Bob Grant, promotes the idea of genetic inferiority. He particularly harps on the inferiority of women. In one program a caller said to him, "You can't take the truth, can you dear?"

Diamond's response: "And you know something? You're a black bitch!"("Single standard on bigotry needed," 1994).

Howard Stern–Syndicated radio, based in Los Angeles, is mean-spirited, tasteless and racist. He was called up short after his "shock jock" jokes on air about the murder of Latino singer Selena. He did apologize to the Hispanic community, but said, "As you know, I am a satirist" (Frankel, 1995).

Rush Limbaugh–Syndicated radio and television, based in New York, is considered the supreme talk show host. Limbaugh has a syndicated show that at one time reached 20 million people a week on 660 radio stations. He calls his listeners "ditto heads," and touts himself as the conservative voice of the people. He says his is "talent on loan from God."

Limbaugh has especially enraged women and calls feminists who believe in abortion "femi-nazis." He says women were doing quite well in this country before feminism came along. A typical "Rushism" is "I love the Women's Movement, especially when I'm walking behind it" (Corliss, 1995).

Columnist Molly Ivins (1995), in an article in *Mother Jones,* said, "Instead of picking on someone his own size, Rush consistently targets dead people, little girls, and the homeless—none of whom can fight back.

"I should explain that I am not without bias in this matter. I have been attacked by Rush Limbaugh on the air, an experience somewhat akin to being gummed by a newt. It doesn't actually hurt, but it leaves you with slimy stuff on your ankle" (Ivins, 1995).

The power of broadcast media should be recognized. Almost every American has access daily to radio and television. This broadcast power also can be used for promoting diversity, harmony and representation in covering the community.

Walter Cronkite (1996), highly respected broadcast reporter of the 20th century, said, "There is a powerful lot of junk on our airwaves. . . . But along with the trash, there is a lot that is good" (p. 382).

Journalists have the opportunity to shape broadcast decisions by clearly making diversity decisions about their work. Television has a responsibility to the public to cover the community and to show accurate images and a wide range of images to viewers. Radio journalists should be promoting harmony and unity among races and genders rather than airing the worst of human interaction.

WORKING THE BEAT

Exercises

1. Monitor one and one-half hours of television prime time news (Monday through Friday nights). You can limit your survey to the networks: ABC, CBS and NBC or you may add CNN and Fox. Each student should choose one to monitor. Balance the number of monitors evenly among the networks. All students will monitor the same week.

Create summary sheets for the news, putting these topics across the top of the sheets: **News Anchor/Reporter** (male, female, minority?), **Story Topic** (about male, female, minority or other?), **Story Newsmaker** (male, female, minority or other?), **Story Format** (straight news or feature), and **Comments**: (good place to record stereotypes, images, word choice or omission and quotations).

Analyze your findings: What are the percentages of male, female and minority anchors/reporters? What percentage of stories are about males, females or minorities? Break this into straight news stories and feature stories. Who are the newsmakers?—give percentages. Did you find instances of stereotypes, poor word choice or omission from stories? What were

(continued)

WORKING THE BEAT (continued)

typical images of women and minorities in television filming? Which of your local affiliates had the best showing of women and minorities? Which has the best diversity record, local or national news?

Compile your class findings and share these with other journalism and communications classes and diversity groups on campus. Share your findings with the news managers of the networks you monitored.

2. Divide the class into five-member groups. Each group will come up with a list of 10 ways television can improve the news. Each group reports to the class. Compile a class list of the 10 best ways television news can be improved. Discuss who has the power to make these changes. Include this list with your findings in Exercise 1 when you send them or present them to the news managers.

3. Research three women and/or minority television news personalities. Write an article profiling their lives. Include: How have their paths been similar and how different? How has their work contributed to the progress of women and minorities in television news? What was their strongest influence professionally? What advice do they give for covering the news?

4. Invite a local woman and/or minority television or radio news personality to speak to the class. Ask the speaker to include among the speech topics: What have been your experiences as a woman and/or minority in the news media? Each student will write a feature article covering the speech.

5. Listen to a radio talk show and a radio news program. Write an analysis of the differences. Many people believe what they hear on talk shows is the news and the truth. Explain the power of this medium and discuss the responsibility of the airways to the public. Document your assignment with the name, time and date of the programs you monitored. Include statistics, examples and quotations in your analysis.

8 Practicing Diversity in Public Relations and Advertising

$\blacklozenge$

Public relations and advertising are two of the fastest growing fields in communications. In the 1990s, journalism trade magazines, such as *Quill*, reported the majority of journalism and communication majors went into these two fields. New graduates, as well as veteran media professionals, are attracted to corporate dazzle as well as to the frequently generous salaries in comparison to those in newspapers, radio or television.

John D. Rockefeller once said, "The ability to deal with people is as purchasable a commodity as sugar and coffee. And I pay more for that ability than for any other under the sun" (Acker, 1992).

Looking at Public Relations

An added attraction for journalists is the fact that an enormous amount of news appearing in each day's papers comes from public relations writers. Experts say as much as 80 percent. Yet, the field of public relations is full of ambivalence. Media people who go from news to PR are accused of "going over to the other side."

PR professionals are accused of producing "flack" because the view they present puts the nonprofit agency, the government agency and the private company in a positive light.

Since Edward Bernays, the Father of Public Relations, began the profession in the 1920s, the field has changed considerably. Strict ethical codes are embraced by professionals. Both reporters and PR specialists are persuaders and providers of news. They are advocates with a professional's sense of obligation to truth and fairness. The role of advocate and information source requires applied ethics for the clients as well as for the publics they serve (Christians, Flacker and Rotzoll, "Persuasion and Public Relations," 1995).

◆

Looking at Advertising

Going into the profession of advertising calls for using the most persuasive techniques known to society. With this power should go the ethics required to regulate any tendency to defame or damage competitors and the ethics to regulate any tendency to falsify information or objectify people. Advertising is the art of showing the public what you are selling and presenting it in a persuasive, positive light. Public relations is image-building, whereas advertising is marketing and selling. Both fields are incredibly powerful. Both fields are concerned with mass persuasion.

Ethical Guidelines and Principles of Persuasion

Both PR and advertising use professional codes of ethics. If you read these codes carefully, the professional is held to the same standards as a print or broadcast journalist. It follows then, that diversity of community should be practiced in PR and in advertising.

PR and advertising use mass media to reach large audiences, yet the persuasiveness of their techniques sometimes reaches audiences who could be damaged by the messages. Television is the most indiscriminate of the mass media. It reaches the rich and the poor, all ethnic and racial groups, all religions, each gender and sexual orientation and those who have disabilities. Sometimes advertisers design a message for the affluent, for example, yet it also reaches the poor. Critics raise ethical issues about the fallout influence on those who could be damaged. For example, Harvard economist Juliet Schor analyzed TV watcher spending habits in 1998. Her findings show that "for each hour a week spent watching television, an additional $208 a year is spent. Sitting in front of the TV five extra hours a week raises your yearly spending by about $1,000."

Schor says it's not just the ads that are getting us to buy more, it's the lifestyles depicted that inflate our sense of what's normal. She says she sees the affluence portrayed on television as one of the reasons for "competitive consumption" that's wrecking many household finances (Marlowe, 1998).

Another important issue concerns the tobacco industry, which has suffered under the social health demands that have restricted sales and generated law suits. Tobacco companies have scrambled to pick up the losses and are accused of targeting young people with symbols such as "Joe Camel" in order to compel a new generation to smoke (Christians, Flacker and Rotzoll, "Persuasion and Advertising," 1995).

The principles of persuasion include creating a need within the viewer, the listener or the reader. Leaders in PR and advertising contend that the public is intelligent enough to be discerning and will choose what is appropriate for themselves. On the other side, those carrying the banner of special audiences contend the system is unfair to their constituencies and therefore must change. Children's advocates rightly complain of advertising campaigns on Saturday morning that "sell" children on certain toys and breakfast cereals. Women's groups unite against the sexy stereotypes of women as objects to be used to sell products and services, and minorities complain about being omitted from advertising.

So how do you persuade and still keep diverse community ethics? Let's examine public relations and advertising separately.

Practicing Diversity in Public Relations

PR writing uses news releases, newsletters, brochures, public service announcements, speeches and other business writing to get its message over. In writing these, practitioners must be socially aware of the publics they serve. Following are some ways to practice diversity while practicing public relations:

1. Most PR efforts are not aimed at the general public, but at the special interest groups they target. Know this group inside out. Examine the demographics and the psychographics of the group. Go where this particular group lives, works and plays.

2. Design the message to fit the target audience. Just because a group's first language is not English, don't assume they don't know correct English. What are your word choices? What is your goal? Never put down another group or individuals to make your point. Let the message stand on its merit.

3. Use proper channels to deliver the message to the target audience. Will you use a news release, a newsletter, a brochure, a flyer, a public service announcement, a speech or an advertisement to reach the audience? A news release to a senior newspaper will reach older people, but it will not necessarily reach Asian or Cuban older people.

4. Know the media. Would several radio spots hit your target audience? Would a timely news release generate a newspaper article or television news spot?

Would an article aimed at Latino women be better placed in *Latino* or the local newspaper, or would that message be better channeled through an audience-targeted radio station?

5. Cultivate media contacts who are appropriate to the section of the media you want to reach and who are appropriate to the audience you want to reach. Generate a media list for contact in your locale. Ask minority and women reporters' and editors' advice on how to reach their readers and viewers.

6. Develop news judgment as it relates to newsworthiness. Maybe to you and your Korean client it's interesting that they're opening a new restaurant, but why would the general public be interested? Make it newsworthy by including how many Korean restaurants are in the area, how many people they hire, approximately how many people in the city eat at these restaurants. Make it newsworthy by creating an authentic Korean opening for the restaurant with community leaders. Invite a Korean celebrity to participate and ask your client to donate the first day's proceeds to the Asian Community Center for Children.

7. Socially cultivate community leaders from all groups. Attend their meetings, join professional groups where they belong and generate a diversity list from the community. Networking is essential in public relations. Having a diversity contact list guarantees you will have access to diversity opinions and thereby represent the community.

8. Develop your own individual code of ethics: always tell the truth, be responsible and responsive to the media and to the public, stand firm against campaigns that damage others and work on a reputation of integrity so that the community knows that you and your agency cannot be bought. Discover what the different special groups in your community consider honorable.

9. Help your clients and the public develop trust in you by being honest and reliable. Do what you say you'll do. Be responsible by showing up on time, by keeping your word, and remembering that trust is built over a period of time.

10. Always ask the ultimate question: Who will it help? Who will it harm? Public relations should be the business of helping people: clients and the community.

Developing Projects and Events

Every endeavor in public relations should follow a simple pattern: conduct a needs assessment, plan what you're going to do, do it, and evaluate the project. What went right? What could you do better next time? At each point in this basic process, think of the diversity guidelines.

In the needs assessment include not only your client managers, but the mini-groups within the target audience. Sometimes PR professionals miss the mark because they think we know what people want. Never assume; always know before you begin.

Planning should include all levels of participants: your staff, the client's staff, representatives of the target audience and community representatives. Wal-Mart has had to overcome all sorts of PR problems because of its habit of going into small communities, buying cheap land and opening a store. Small community businesses that are run out of business have protested enough to keep Wal-Mart out of some communities. The more affluent public supports the small community stores and the poor are neglected. So, if you were doing public relations for Wal-Mart, consider these questions: What would be the advantages to the affluent and to the small store owners, as well as to those in the community? Who needs to buy their products at a reasonable rate?

Doing the project involves including all of the above in the actual production of the event. When people agree to be a part of something, they feel it becomes a part of them, and they support it. Why would a university have faculty sit down with students and plan the curriculum? Because the students have insights that only they can offer as to their needs for the future. College and university officials all over the country could learn and benefit from this basic principle.

And last, always evaluate results of a project or campaign. Don't keep inventing the wheel. Everything you do in public relations can be examined for the gold you've mined from that particular project. If it works, try it again. What doesn't work may not be worthless, but it may be used in another kind of project. Never neglect to evaluate when you've finished a project. This also is a report to your client about what services you have provided. And remember, *proactive* public relations— building goodwill all along—is worth a thousand *reactive* moves—acting on crisis, after the fact.

Practicing Diversity in Advertising

Advertising is simply selling. In a democratic society that promotes competition, advertising is a necessity so sellers can attract buyers to their goods and services. The world of advertising rewards creativity and individuality. Listen to your own instincts and inspiration.

Whereas public relations sells goodwill, advertising sells commodities. As much care should be taken in advertising as in public relations to be culturally sensitive to community and special group needs. Ad writers should know just as much about their audience as newspaper journalists should know about their community.

Taco Bell chain ran television spots in 1993 urging consumers to "Run for the Border." The campaign was created by Chicago-based Foote, Cone, and Belding. The campaign ran African "savages" to represent "wild" tacos. African American consumers complained in great numbers, and Mexican Americans said the "Run for the Border" slogan was condescending since Mexican immigrants are blamed for economic depression and unemployment. In border states such as Texas, New Mexico and California, they are already the target of racism. The result of this campaign caused boycotts of Taco Bell, especially in southwestern states where they are dealing with border problems.

Just as the image seemed ruined beyond repair, Taco Bell began recovering with the chihuahua ads, showing first a willful chihuahua, leaving behind a charming, doggie lover to seek his tacos: "Yo quiero Taco Bell." The campaign continued after some complaints from Mexican Americans, yet pretty much charmed the public with the chihuahua's beret-clad, Che Guevara-like appearance as leading the revolution. He became a South American doggie!

As Godzilla came to the big screen, Taco Bell tied its advertising to the film and the chihuahua is seen trying to trap Godzilla with some tacos in a pasteboard box. Next comes Godzilla and the chihuahua as pals, coming up to a Taco Bell drive-in, buying dozens and dozens of drinks for Godzilla.

Lisa Balmaseda (1992), a columnist for the Miami Herald, says, "Hard as I try to search for larger political meaning at Taco Bell, I keep coming back to the same two points: It's a dog. And it's a taco."

Dottie Enrico, *USA Today* advertising specialist, says that mean-spirited advertising such as comparison ads are out. She says humor is in, with the most popular being the Budweiser frogs, the Michelin babies and the milk processors' "Got Milk" ads.

The National Fluid Milk Processor Promotion Board spent more than $35 million in 1997 at approximately 50 publications to run the milk mustache ads. This campaign has been wildly successful for a print campaign and two thirds of the public polled who had seen the ads said they were effective. The ads show men, women and minorities with their milk mustaches (Enrico, 1997).

One of the not so successful ad campaigns was the Reebok KMX 2 Triple O show sneakers that sell for $150. Heater of Boston designed the television ad that begins with a rap song about Allen Iverson's (Philadelphia 76ers) "spats with the system." Iverson is a pro basketball player who was arrested for gun possession and put on three years' probation. A marijuana possession charge was dropped as part of his plea agreement.

According to Reebok's worldwide advertising director John Wardley, the ad was aimed at urban teens and planned to be aired on MTV, the Black Entertainment Network and during NBA broadcasts. He said the ad was written as a show of support for Iverson. Critics said that even though Iverson was named Rookie of the Year, he's not a good role model for young people. Reebok wisely decided not to air the ad ("Reebok Stumbles Badly With DMX," 1997).

Women and Minority
Dollars Influence Advertising

Unfortunately, money drives much social change, and industry is finally realizing that cultural sensitivity pays off. In 1998, *The Economist* magazine reported on the nation's fastest-growing population: "Latinos have the highest rate of male participation in the labor force, the lowest use of public assistance and the highest rate of family formation. . . . Although most arrive (as immigrants) with no capital and take rock-bottom jobs, they are reaching the middle class in increasingly large numbers" (Balmaseda, 1998).

As the population and buying power of Latinos increase in the United States, many companies are spending more to reach this market. The top 50 advertisers in the Latino market spent an estimated $392.8 million (total advertising) in 1997. The top five were Procter & Gamble; AT&T; Sears, Roebuck; General Motors; and MCI Communications.

Sears has been wooing the Latino customer for years. It publishes a Latino magazine that's mailed to 700,000 households—crammed with Sears ads. On Spanish-language TV, it's unusual for a few hours to pass without seeing a Sears spot (Kirkpatrick, 1998).

Fashion designer Tommy Hilfiger ran into trouble when anonymous critics produced a negative cyberspace campaign and blasted him as racist because of some remarks he made about his line of clothing. He said he does not make his clothes specifically for black people.

Snoop Doggy Dogg and Sadat Z of Grand Nubian are among Hilfiger's fans. A Hilfiger spokesperson said the company did not want their products to be identified with urban black youth, and that's the reason blacks are not targeted in ads (all white models), even though blacks buy a high percentage of their products.

After the criticism, Hilfiger thanked blacks for their support and in response has hired more African designers and now features black models prominently in his ads and shows. The anti-Hilfiger campaign from consumers was damaging, and Hilfiger launched an e-mail blitz to set the record straight ("Designer Hilfiger," 1997).

African Americans face many forms of discrimination in advertisements themselves. They are often subordinated to both male and female whites in ads, and many black women portrayed as beautiful are those who have lightened their skin. Media critic Jean Kilbourne says, "The message here is about power and superiority of men over women and white over black" (Copeland, 1996).

Kilbourne is internationally known and has traveled the country for more than two decades discussing advertisements and presenting slide shows to universities, community groups and businesses. Her message is simple: advertisements have power and strongly influence our culture.

She says the subliminal effects of negative images in the mass media are more "pervasive and persuasive" than any other force in society in shaping our ideas and attitudes about love, sex, success, popularity and normalcy. Kilbourne points out that the $160 billion advertising industry, by bombarding us every waking minute of our lives with images and messages, is one of the most powerful educational tools in society. She says the average American is exposed to 3,000 ads per day.

Kilbourn adds, "Women are made to feel ashamed or guilty if they do not live up to the flawless, thin, beautiful, young, sexy, babyish and inhumanely perfect standard set by female models in ads. However, 95 percent of all women cannot possibly live up to these expectations; and, as a result, eating disorders, low self-esteem and anxiety are common among women" (Copeland, 1996).

Other special groups feel they suffer from advertisements. Laura Hershey, a columnist for the *Denver Post* and also a woman disabled by a neuromuscular condition, lashed out at what she calls the Jerry Lewis sideshow for the Muscular Dystrophy Association. She asks for "pity campaigns for people with disabilities" to stop.

Hershey describes the black-and-white television ads commissioned by the National Multiple Sclerosis Society that showed women blindfolded, bodies slouching, with arms wrapped in rope and chains.

She says, "With their [the ads] violent, pseudo-pornographic images, the ads reinforce stereotypes about both gender and disability, perpetuating the notion that a woman with a disability is naturally, inescapably helpless—the perfect victim" (Hershey, 1995).

Targeting age groups can become a diversity issue in advertisements. R.J. Reynolds Tobacco Company (RJR) has learned that the hard way. Court evidence convinced a jury that RJR targeted teens for tobacco sales. Because of court decisions, RJR will pay more than $386 billion over a 25-year period and curb their marketing practices. Because of the rising alarm over lung cancer and because of insider leaks from tobacco companies, Attorney General Janet Reno led an investigation into marketing practices.

The Joe Camel cartoon debuted in France and was brought to the United States in 1987. Camel rose to become the No. 2 brand among teenagers, and RJR continued to target teens.

In a California suit against the company, San Francisco attorney Louise Renne said, "The documents [marketing documents from RJR] make clear the extent to which RJR and other tobacco companies are targeting our kids. If you can get a young person to smoke before they're 18, they are then hooked for life" (Neergaard, 1998).

The Associated Press reported, "The company's strategy included a direct advertising appeal to the younger habits and to true-to-life young adult situations. The ads were to run in magazines, such as *Sports Illustrated*, that are widely read by teens. Efforts to target young males specifically included sponsoring sports car racing and developing T-shirts and other paraphernalia that could provide a million walking billboards for their brands" (Neergaard, 1998).

Advertising today is global, as is public relations. Not only must advertisers be culturally sensitive in the United States, but they must carry through in other countries. If you plan to enter either of these fields, study language and international business.

Pepsi created an amusing *faux pas* when they ran their "Come Alive with the Pepsi Generation." When Pepsi-Cola invaded the huge Chinese and German markets, the effort initially fizzled. The product's slogan was rendered into Chinese as "Pepsi Brings Back Your Dead Ancestors," and its translation into German was, "Come Out of the Grave with Pepsi" ("Language Translation," 1995).

What Is Good Advertising?

First, it is socially responsible. If you plan a career in advertising, you must clearly define your ethics and practices. The persuasive techniques are so powerful that they can be used for good or evil.

Good advertising offers a benefit or reward for reading. Ad copy must be easily understood, and it should be honest and believable. It informs and motivates. Creative ad copy is memorable. It should be short.

Good advertising must be appropriate to the product or service. It must work hand in hand with public relations to reflect favorably on the overall image of the advertiser. And, of course, good advertising must succeed in its planned objectives (Hafer and White, 1988).

Author Eric Clark (1990) in his book *The Want Makers* says, "Advertising may be a key ingredient of a competitive economy, but as advertising budgets become ever more mega, it is also increasingly a weapon that benefits the large at the expense of the small. . . . More control over advertising is vital, at the risk even of the great evil, bureaucracy. . . . Advertising has many positive features. It is needed to spread useful information. It has energy and extravagance. It can be fun—most of us have favorite ads that actually engender affection. But it is also a big, powerful, highly talented and immensely wealthy industry."

WORKING THE BEAT

Exercises

1. Collect five news releases from public relations firms or from businesses that have a public relations department. You can go to local businesses or collect five from Internet sources. Write an analysis of these releases answering these questions and others that you generate as you are doing the analysis: Who releases this news? Are they government agencies, private businesses or nonprofit agencies? Do they really have a "news" release, or is this just a publicity release or a media advisory? How could they have made this a real community news story if it isn't? What is the benefit to the agency who released this information? What is the benefit to the community? Rewrite the longest release to one page.

2. Invite a public relations professional and an advertising executive to class for a panel discussion of the differences between public relations and advertising. Ask them each to bring samples of actual news releases and advertisements. Distribute copies to the class. Write an article for the campus newspaper about the information that came from this event.

3. Monitor one and one-half hours of prime-time (Monday through Friday nights) news television commercials. Prime-time is the most expensive to advertisers because this time slot is watched by more people. Create a tally sheet that has these topics across the top of the page: **Product or Service, Aimed at Men or Women? Omission, Word Choice, Stereotype, Comments:** Tally the numbers of products for men, for women.

Tally how many commercials omitted obvious people; for example, how many women and minorities were represented in these commercials? Who were the lead actors? Did you find any word choices that might offend, denigrate or patronize women or minorities? Did you see any stereotypes of diversity groups? How many voice-overs were men, and how many were women? In the comments section, record your impressions and any quotations that validate your points. Write an analysis of the monitoring project above.

4. Clip five magazine advertisements. Make a poster board collage of the ads. Analyze each by examining: Who is portrayed? What are the appeals of the advertisement? Did you find any stereotypical images in the ads? Who is the target audience for these ads? How could you make the ads better, thinking in terms of meeting a diversity market? Write up your analysis. Discuss your findings in class.

5. Write a print and broadcast advertisement for a new man's hand lotion. Give it a name. Visualize how you would present it in print with the copy. How would you overcome male resistance? What would be your

WORKING THE BEAT (continued)

appeal? How would you present the same advertisement for a television commercial? Present your advertisement to the class. Cut out magazine pictures to represent your visual.

6. Find five Internet advertisements and analyze them by word appeal, visual appeal and diversity issues. Discuss how they are different from television advertisements.

9 Going to the Source

———————◆———————

Following are some valuable professional guidelines for reporting on different races, multicultural groups, the disabled, different lifestyles, older adults and women. Even though the information in this chapter comes from the diverse groups themselves, remember always to ask the interviewee how he or she wants to be identified.

As a writer, photographer or artist, your job is to be aware of covering your community. In whichever state or city you work, urban or rural, you need to be aware of the different groups to whom you are writing as well as about whom you are writing. As a media professional, you will find it helpful to put together a diversity resource notebook of names and groups involved *in your community*. This will guide you in writing or portraying this special group.

———————◆———————

The selected guidelines in this chapter are listed by groups in alphabetical order: The terms used are those suggested by the national journalists', media organizations and publicity offices of these special interest groups.

Covering African Americans/Blacks

1. *African American* or *black* is preferred. Sometimes, *people of color* is used. Ask the interviewee and those involved in the story how they want to be identified. The words *Negro, nigger* and *colored* are derogatory.

2. Consider stories that portray African Americans in all facets of life. Do blacks often appear in articles about crime, sports and entertainment but rarely in articles about business, politics or science? Write more follow-up stories after crimes involving black people. Describe how a star baseball player is volunteering for a local boys club, for example.

3. Avoid "Gee Whiz" stories about African Americans that show astonishment that blacks could accomplish whatever. A better approach is to consider stories about black people who have made it because they did all the things any other hardworking, motivated individual would do to get ahead.

4. Don't limit stories about blacks to Black History Month or to an annual series on the anniversary of a riot.

5. Be specific when describing a black person. If the person is not American, specify the nationality. OK: He is an African. Better: He is a Ghanian. OK: She is a West Indian. Better: She is Jamaican.

6. Avoid using *ghetto* to describe sections where minorities or the poor live. Specify the particular community—Harlem. Inner city is also used to label areas where there are large minority populations, leaving a negative perception.

7. No single person speaks for all black people. Continually meet and cultivate new sources.

8. Talk with African Americans in a variety of settings. Go to traditional meetings such as churches, but also drop in and talk to people in barber shops and the corner store.

9. In photos and graphics blacks are often shown in pain, crying, dancing, singing or shooting basketballs. Consider including blacks in art festivals, in classrooms, in hospital operating rooms and in libraries (Dalton, 1994; Featherstone, 1995; Irby, 1995; *News Watch*, 1994).

Covering Asian Americans

Asian Pacific Americans are a fast-growing ethnic minority in America; their numbers have more than doubled since 1970. Despite this growth, the news media's knowledge about Asian Americans lags.

There are disturbing trends—rising anti-Asian violence, Japan-bashing, escalating racial tensions and stagnating affirmative action efforts. With these existing problems it is even more important for media to "get it right" when covering Asian Pacific Americans. There are several key problems that tend to mar news coverage of this group:

1. *Stereotypes* — One common stereotype of Asian Americans is the "model or super minority" myth. This says that Asian Americans are all successful, well-educated and immune from any of the social problems that affect other communities of color, such as poverty, drug abuse, lack of health coverage or civil rights violations. This pits Asian Americans against other minority groups.

Another spin on this myth is that "all Asians are alike," ignoring the fact that people from 17 specific Asian groups and eight Pacific Islander groups live in the United States. Each group and each individual is different.

The flip side of the "model minority" myth is that Asian Americans are forever foreigners in the United States. They are portrayed as having funny accents and exotic customs. Or they are depicted as aggressive, war-hungry invaders taking over America. Two of the most powerful media images to emerge from the Los Angeles riots were the photographs of Uzi-toting Korean American merchants, guarding their shops, and of shopkeeper Soon Ja Du shooting a suspected black shoplifter.

2. *Loaded Words* — Asians are no longer called *Oriental,* but *Asian American* or specifically by their country or group. For example, Korean American, Chinese American, or Japanese American. Rugs are oriental.

Words such as *clever, inscrutable* or *shrewd,* though positive, can conjure up stereotypes of Asian Americans as mindless automatons. Terms like *China doll* and *dragon lady* belittle Asian American women, young and old, respectively. These terms are stereotypical and sexist.

3. *Loaded Images* — Cartoonists and artists should avoid depicting Asians with buck teeth, slanted eyes and/or big, round eyeglasses, such as was done in World War II propaganda images. The film industry's Charlie Chan and Kung Fu images are just as offensive.

4. *Ethnic Slurs* — Words such as *Japs, Nips, Chinks, Chinaman, Gooks* and *Nippers* are racial slurs and should not be used. When a public official uses words such as these, get a reaction quote from a leader in the Asian American community.

5. *Media Insensitivity* — Asian Americans are frequently ignored by the news media as the subject of stories and as sources. Invisibility can be as dangerous as stereotypes and racial slurs. By ignoring Asian American stories and voices, the media perpetuate the belief that they are outside the mainstream of United States life and that their perspectives do not matter. Newspapers in communities with sizable Asian American populations should consider the community a beat.

6. *Military Metaphors* — Use caution when using military metaphors about Asian Pacific Americans and some international issues such as trade. Phrases such as *war, invasion* and *Pearl Harbor* are often used to portray Asian Americans as an invading force, again perpetuating the mistaken belief that they are outsiders taking over the country. The terms reinforce an "us versus them" attitude, which often serves to exacerbate racial tensions and hate crimes (ASNE, 1993; Moon, 1996; Nakamura, 1995; *News Watch*, 1994; *The Asian American Handbook*, 1991).

Covering People With Disabilities

The enactment of the Americans with Disabilities Act has increased sensitivity about people with disabilities. Following are some considerations when covering people with disabilities:

1. Avoid pity stories. People with disabilities aren't helpless.

2. Don't always choose the angle of the super hero in the story. People with disabilities are just like everyone else except they live with some kind of disability. "Wow" stories are unconsciously insulting. These stories imply that doing something that is ordinary for most people is extraordinary for someone who has a disability, and this may not be so.

3. Use terms that focus on the people, not on the disability. For example, use *a person with cerebral palsy* rather than a *CP*; use *people who are deaf or hearing impaired* rather than *the deaf.*

4. Don't mention a person's disability unless it is relevant to the story.

5. Photographers should talk with the person with disabilities to obtain the subject's ideas about portrayal that is positive or neutral.

6. Be careful of terms used for those with disabilities: use *disabled* rather than *handicapped.* Handicapped comes from a time when social welfare consisted of those with disabilities begging on a street corner with their cap in their hand to catch the coins. Don't use: blind, deaf and dumb, crippled, she is a vegetable.

7. When interviewing a person with disabilities, allow plenty of time. Treat him or her as a person who has many qualities in addition to a disability. Learn what the person can do, and don't show amazement at his or her accomplishments.

8. Make direct eye contact with the interviewee and don't raise your voice unless asked to. Don't assume someone with a disability is hard of hearing or has other disabilities. Ask the person about issues that affect the disabled, which will lead you to many other stories (ASNE, 1993; ASNE, 1990).

Covering Gay-Related Stories

1. Gay people prefer to be called *gay,* not *homosexuals. Gay* has been the decided word for this community since 1969.

2. Inanimate objects do not have sexual orientation. For instance, a newspaper such as the *Washington Blade,* is not a homosexual newspaper, it is a newspaper for the gay community.

3. Openly gay people are not admitted homosexuals or known homosexuals. They are openly gay.

4. Homosexuals are not at high risk for AIDS. Lesbians are homosexual but are not at high risk for AIDS—in fact, they are at the very least risk. Sexually active gay men is a better term to identify this particular risk group.

5. Most social scientists today agree that sexual attraction is probably a product of both genetics and environment. A person does not grow up and then somewhere along the line simply choose to be attracted to a person of the opposite or of the same sex. Therefore, *sexual orientation* is a more accurate description than *sexual preference* when referring to the sexual attraction that motivates people.

6. Obituaries should reflect reality. A reporter does not verify a spouse to list them in a person's obituary; thus, a long-time partner

or companion should be treated in the same fair way (ASNE, 1993; Keen, 1987).

Covering Latinos/Hispanics

The term *Latino* describes those Spanish-speaking people who are from Latin America. The term *Hispanic* describes Spanish-speaking people. Many use the terms interchangeably, yet Mexican Americans, who make up a high percentage of the ethnic populations in the United States, are by definition *Hispanic*.

George Ramos is *The Los Angeles Times* Senior Writer for Latino Affairs and has spent years developing his skills in reporting Latinos or Hispanics. Ramos is the son of illegal immigrants from Mexico. His parents called themselves Mexican Americans, yet he calls himself Chicano and an American of Mexican descent. He says this is common for second-generation immigrants.

The Los Angeles Times has a 20 percent Latino readership. These incorporate Mexicans, Cubans, Puerto Ricans, Salvadorians, Argentines, Dominicans and so forth. Los Angeles, the community, has an approximately 46 percent Latino population.

Ramos says that each group and each individual must be studied so that misconceptions don't occur. He says that about 7 or 8 out of every 10 Mexicans are Democrats because their reason for coming to this country was economic betterment. Therefore, many of them are interested in social issues such as health, immigration laws, education and welfare.

In contrast, Ramos says many Cuban Americans are Republicans because they were the moneyed and business people who came to this country to escape political oppression. Many of them are wealthy and are interested in capitalism and international affairs, such as what is the United States going to do about Castro.

One striking example of stereotyping, says Ramos, is the image of the illegal immigrant. He says, "Close your eyes and visualize a picture of an illegal alien. What most people see is a small, dark individual, which equates to a Mexican or a South American. Yet, of the 4 million illegals in this country, only about 40 percent are Latinos. The others are mostly on tourist visas and stayed illegally."

Other Considerations When Covering Hispanics

1. Don't try to lump holidays together. Cinco de Mayo is a uniquely Mexican holiday, which is of little importance to Cubans or Salvadorians.
2. Even though the government uses the term *illegal alien*, the National Association of Hispanic Journalists has barred its usage. Many feel that such terms are pejorative, not only by those to whom they are applied but also to others of the same ethnic and national backgrounds who are in the United States legally. The recommended term is *illegal immigrants* or *undocumented immigrants.*
3. Long-time stereotypes of Mexicans should be avoided: the lazy worker needing his siesta; the Mexican driving his Chevy truck; the Frito Bandito image; the broken English responses such as "jes"; the colorful, hard-drinking people who party all the time and have many children because of their Catholic heritage. And remember, all Hispanics are not Mexican Americans.
4. The cheapest way for news agencies to avoid inaccurate and insensitive reporting is to hire bilingual and bicultural reporters and editors.
5. If you do not speak the language, use an interpreter.
6. Diversity is an essential news value that must be cultivated. It takes special effort on the part of the reporter to develop awareness to the various cultures within this culture. Covering the community means giving everyone an equal chance, which is the essence of fairness and balance (ASNE, 1993; Featherstone, 1995; Irby, 1995; Ramos, 1996; Takaki, 1993; ASNE, *The Multicultural Newsroom*, 1993).

Covering Native Americans/American Indians

1. Be careful of using and reinforcing stereotypes through such words as *warpath, warriors, scalping* or *savages*. This includes using Indians as "mascots." This trivializes them as human beings and makes it easier to minimize the importance of Native American concerns.
2. Don't misuse Indian-derivative words such as *powwow*. To Native Americans a *powwow* is not just a meeting but a spiritual gathering with many cultural implications. Other words and phrases that have crept into common usage are *low man on the totem pole, wampum* and

squaw. This last word for a woman is particularly offensive because it is derived from an Algonquin language term for female genitalia.

3. Be careful when reporting on legal decisions. While the verbs *assigned* and *allowed* are used commonly, it is offensive to Native Americans to read about their rights being *allowed* when they were never legally relinquished. It is better to use verbs such as *upheld* treaty rights or *recognized* the authority of treaty agreements.

4. It is inaccurate to use the term American Indian when collectively referring to the aboriginal peoples of the United States, for it excludes some Alaska Native groups, including Inuit and Aleut peoples, who are not Indians. Use instead the name of the tribe being described.

5. Omission is strong in media coverage of Native Americans just as it is in covering other minorities and women. Native Americans should not always be reported on as museum pieces of a dying culture. They have ordinary lives as everyone else and are not always at the center of some treaty dispute with the government.

6. Be sensitive to holidays that are derogatory to Native Americans. They are not shown in a good light by Columbus Day, where the country celebrates its invasion by Europeans. And remember, Thanksgiving is a day of solemnity and sadness for many Native Americans.

7. Photographers should be aware of the visual images they give of Native Americans. They are not all victims of poverty and alcoholism. Some Native Americans resent seeing little children wearing colorful, feathered headbands, which to the Native American is a sacred token given only to those who have done exceptional deeds. Seeing the sports spectators giving the *tomahawk chop* is derogatory.

8. Quote tribal and community leaders. Don't always choose the government official as the primary source of tribal policy and information (ASNE, 1993; Featherstone, 1995; *News Watch*, 1994; Takaki, 1993; ASNE, *The Multicultural Newsroom*, 1993).

Covering Older Adults

1. The preferred terms to use are *older adults* or *mature adults*. Some do not like to be called seniors or senior citizens for to them it may sound like jargon, such as "gals" for "women."

2. When writing about older adults in news stories, just use their age:

"Jose Sanchez, 65, was a witness to the drive-by shooting."

Not:

> "Senior citizen Jose Sanchez, 65, was a witness to the drive-by shooting."

Labeling someone implies that his age has something to do with the story.

3. During an interview with an older adult, talk in a natural voice. All older adults are not hearing impaired. If they tell you they are, sit directly in front of them, talk slower and louder and enunciate your words carefully. Many people who are hard of hearing read lips to an extent. Older adults complain frequently that younger people talk too fast.

4. Do not be patronizing. Be respectful. Age does not naturally bring on senility. The interviewee may or may not have a better education than you do, and it's a given he or she has more life education than you do.

5. Be aware of issues of interest to mature adults. Many are on a limited income, and because of longer life span, worry that their money may run out before death. Many are terrified of crime and rightly so, and many have health problems, which brings up other issues such as transportation, insurance, medical choices, drug costs, family and friend support, and housing.

6. Be patient. Older adults may take longer to get around, to respond and to interview. One reason for this is the culture in which they were raised. Many come from a time when any visitor was offered refreshment, so you may have to be sociable before you get down to business. To gain confidence, you need to be sensitive to this.

7. Many older immigrant adults are mistrustful of outsiders, especially law enforcement, social workers or those in authority. Your community contact or a family member or friend may have to introduce you. Some of these immigrants have come from a country where they experienced executions, where neighbors turned in neighbors to the government, and where their survival depended on not telling everything they know.

8. Don't always portray older adults as victims. It has become a stereotype. Equally extreme is the marathon runner. Both of these images are at opposite ends of reality. Most older adults are doing ordinary things that everyone does.

9. Artists and photographers should portray older adults as they do younger adults. Avoid older adult stereotypes: victims in wheelchairs,

the "dirty old man" leering at a beautiful woman, the "crazy old woman" surrounded by her 15 cats.

10. Be aware of the fact that many older people are lonely and some are depressed because their friends are dying, and they experience more and more limitations.

11. Be aware that the young divulge information quite soon compared to older adults who were raised in an era when they were taught, "Don't air your dirty laundry."

12. Don't liken older adults to children. Yet, the reality is that many older adults, because of health problems and limitations, are focused on their own daily needs (Cullen, 1996; Trask, 1998).

Covering Women

You may wonder why reporters must be sensitive about reporting on women when women are about 52 percent of the population and participate daily in business, government, education and so forth. Yet, the history of women in the United States demonstrates the paternalistic culture brought from Europe. Women had no legal rights and were owned by the male: the father, the husband or the brother protector. Women were not allowed to vote in national elections until 1920.

This history of exclusion has put women in a second-class position, where they are still stuck in some life issues. Sexist terms and attitudes are still rampant in this culture, and the reporter must be especially knowledgeable in not furthering sexism in news stories.

Three major sexist techniques occur with women, just as they do with minorities in mass media. They are omission, stereotypes and word choices. For example, women are in small numbers on front pages in bylines, or as newsmakers or experts. Nancy Woodhull, cochair of Women, Men and Media, says, "There is an act called symbolic annihilation. It means that if the press does not report your existence, for all perception purposes, you do not exist."

Certainly, stereotypes still abound in advertisements, in photographs and in cartoons. From looking at these damaging images, it is obvious that women are sex objects, old crones, bimbos without intelligence and certainly not anyone who has an expert opinion on an important subject.

Word usage about women has improved over the past two decades, but women are still described physically, their age has exaggerated importance because young is desirable and older women suffer from sexist terms as well as from ageist ones.

Guidelines When Writing About Women

1. Spread stories about women throughout every section. There should not be a "women's section" just as there should not be a "Hispanic section."

2. Put important women's concerns, such as day care, sexual harassment, Title IX, inequities and unequal pay, on the front page.

3. Make a list of women who are experts in nontraditional fields and call on them for quotes: engineering, economics, medicine and so forth.

4. Cover women's sports.

5. Identify women by their own activities, not as wife of, mother of or daughter of some male.

6. Avoid adjectives such as *petite, feisty, pushy* or *coy.*

7. Keep a file of female sources for stories that directly affect women, such as breast cancer, abortion and fetal tissue research. Quote women who are experts in these areas. Quote women's organizations on these issues.

8. Women's groups are just as diverse as any others. Don't let one group speak for all women. Women of color and white women have common issues, yet they have great differences in other areas. Be sure women of color and white women are quoted.

9. Photographers, cartoonists and graphic artists should be overly sensitive to the objectionable images of women. When men and women are photographed, place them in equal positions. Women should appear on the front pages. Too many times, media publish or tape the stereotypical image of the old bag lady pushing a shopping cart or the celebrity woman, such as the First Lady, with her mouth open (ASNE, 1993; Featherstone, 1995; Gerhardt, 1995; *Image of Women in Television,* 1974; Moon, 1996; Thomas, 1995).

AN INTERVIEW WITH
AN AIDS REPORTER

Joyce Mitchell, a California AIDS reporter and independent television producer, has become an expert because of her professional and personal work with people with AIDS. She has 25 years' television experience and is an Emmy award-winning producer. Mitchell says that when working at KCRA in Sacramento in 1986, she was assigned as AIDS Lifeline producer to generate an AIDS story a week. She said she began seeing babies and teenagers and women with AIDS and realized that the token AIDS story was barely touching the surface of a much larger health story in society. Through these interview experiences, she says she realized that the "main mission of media is to educate people about this problem."

"The largest growing group of people with AIDS falls within the injection drug use population," says Mitchell. "They can no longer be ignored."

These injection drug users are predominantly male and are spreading the infection to women and children. There are underground needle exchange groups in many communities who are working outside the law to try to slow the spread of HIV. They teach the injection drug users how to clean their drugs and exchange their needles. In many states, needle exchange is illegal.

Mitchell says she has worked with these groups because the story had to be told. She broke the underground needle exchange story on ABC in 1994. She says she has an attorney standing by in case she may ever need one, yet the law tends to look the other way.

Access Sacramento sponsors a User Friendly program on cable that is shown every Friday night at 11 p.m. and is aimed at the injection drug users. It is the only show of its kind. Mitchell says this was aired in New York on cable but failed eventually for lack of support. She says she is producing the programs from a small grant from a university. She freelances independent shows for public television also and for ABC News.

Joyce Mitchell says, "It's a whole new world of reporting happening right now, and there is a huge concern for society. Our young people are at risk. The newest rising numbers in the population with AIDS are people between the ages of 20 and 28 years. That means that they were most likely infected when they were teenagers. We're not doing a good enough job of education."

Media are not doing their part, according to Mitchell. "My biggest frustration is getting people to listen."

AN INTERVIEW WITH AN AIDS REPORTER (continued)

She says that she has had bosses yell at her, "No more AIDS stories."

Media journalists and news directors seem to think this is an old story, particularly in light of the decline in deaths. This is due in part to the triple drug therapies keeping people alive longer. Yet, hepatitus C is also rampant. Hepatitus C is transmitted the same way as HIV. It is a new HIV problem for which there is no cure. Mitchell says that 96 percent of drug users in Sacramento test positive to hepatitus C, and the majority of all drug users now test positive. She says it is easier to get than HIV.

"Another area that society must address related to HIV is money because it costs the community $15,000 a year per person to pay for the triple drug therapies. The costs are prohibitive and each community has that burden. Some kind of regulation will have to be addressed in the future," says Mitchell.

Joyce Mitchell is one individual who is doing her part. From the professional who was assigned the topic in the 1980s to the totally immersed media professional and volunteer today, she puts her message on the line: "Television is the best educational tool. The AIDS story must be revisited at regular intervals" (Mitchell, 1998).

Covering HIV and AIDS

Those suffering from AIDS in our country are shunned just as lepers have been throughout the centuries. The spread of the disease has slowed in the few years since it has been identified, yet prejudice and pain have grown around the problems associated with the families, the health care and the workplaces of these individuals.

Even medical professionals discriminate, and society does nothing to stop this. In an article in the *Boston Globe* (December 26, 1994), Belinda Dunn says she saw five doctors before she found one who was willing to give her a complete examination and felt comfortable enough to look her in the eye. Dunn has AIDS.

In April 1994, a United States District Court in Illinois ordered a physician to treat a Los Angeles man who had been denied a little-known, alternative medicine for hepatitis B because he was infected with HIV. And in the fall of that same year, a federal jury in Ohio awarded $512,000 in damages to the estate of a patient who was refused treatment at a hospital because he had AIDS.

Because of the prejudice associated with AIDS, reporters must be careful in protecting people's privacy and in gathering the facts carefully and accurately about the disease.

Guidelines When Writing About HIV/AIDS

1. Educate yourself on what HIV/AIDS is. There are many health information and support groups that will talk with you or send you materials. Use the most updated information. Start with: www.ama-assn.org and www.aegis.com/topics

2. Protect your individual sources and use pseudonyms if they request this. There is still extreme prejudice and ignorance about the condition. Consider how society dealt with leprosy in the past; this is a similar situation.

3. Most larger communities have hospices, foundations and home care support for people with AIDS. As a reporter, visit and talk with patients, volunteers and medical personnel. Get permission from persons with AIDS to interview them or from whomever has their power of attorney. Always get permission in writing.

4. Use the individual to tell your story. If you can get the readers to identify with the people involved, you can touch them with the information. Anecdotes and scenarios are effective. In the last stages, people with AIDS may not be talking. Describe the conditions and surroundings and interview the caretakers.

5. In each article you write, tell the message of how HIV is spread and how to avoid the infection.

6. Use current health statistics to dispel the myth that only gay men have HIV/AIDS.

7. Publish community resources so the public can contact them for information.

8. Don't limit your research to accepted AMA information; contact underground groups for alternate treatments not accepted by the FDA. The government takes a long time in giving approval, which in most cases is to our advantage; yet those who are dying of AIDS are making themselves guinea pigs for future breakthroughs. This should be reported also.

9. Be cautious about terms used. HIV virus is redundant. The V stands for virus. Don't use "AIDS patient" but a "person with AIDS" or PWA because not all people with AIDS are patients. The old term "IV drug user" has been replaced with "injection drug user" because many don't inject in their veins; they do what they call "skin popping" (Keen, 1987; Mitchell, 1998).

10 Reporters' Resources, Ethics Codes and Laws

———————————————◆———————————————

This resource chapter begins with several codes of ethics of professional organizations that are useful for media. Print, broadcast, public relations and photojournalism ethics are included. Although each speaks to the relevant group within the field, they all carry the same message of reporting the truth, revering accuracy, balancing the message and working for the public benefit. Next is a listing of relevant laws, which govern media and special groups.

Additionally, a listing of professional organizations is included so the writer preparing a story about a special interest group can contact these groups and seek further understanding of the group's cultural beliefs and sensitivity to certain words and phrases. A number of the groups have publications on such topics as writing about disabilities and reporting on minorities.

Several excellent books about online resources are listed, as well as some useful online web sites for journalists.

Last is a listing and descriptions of recognized extremist groups compiled by the Anti-Defamation League. This section should alert the journalists to be cautious about using literature and research from these groups, or for that matter, from any group without double-checking its activities and credentials. Many times the source of information is disguised, and media can be misled into using it.

———————————————◆———————————————

Ethics Codes

Code of Ethics for the Society of
Professional Journalists

SPJ
16 South Jackson St.
Greencastle, IN 46135-1514
765-653-3333
spj@spihq.org

The following is a summary of topics covered in the SPJ Code of
Ethics.

The Society of Professional Journalists believes the duty of journalists is to serve the truth.

We believe the agencies of mass communication are carriers of
public discussion and information, acting on their constitutional man-
date and freedom to learn and report the facts.

We believe those responsibilities carry obligations that require journalists to perform with intelligence, objectivity, accuracy and fairness.

To these ends, we declare acceptance of the standards of practice
here set forth:

    I. RESPONSIBILITY—The public's right to know is the mission of mass
media, and the purpose is to serve the general welfare.

    II. FREEDOM OF THE PRESS—This is an inalienable right of people in
a free society.

    III. ETHICS—Journalists must be free of obligation to any interest other
than the public's right to know the truth.

    IV. ACCURACY AND OBJECTIVITY—Truth is our ultimate goal.

    V. FAIR PLAY—Journalists at all times will show respect for the dignity,
privacy, rights, and well-being of people encountered in the course of
gathering and presenting the news.

    VI. PLEDGE—Adherence to this code is intended to preserve and streng-
then the bond of mutual trust and respect between American journalists and the American people.

The Society shall—by programs of education and other means—encourage individual journalists to adhere to these tenets and shall encourage journalistic publications and broadcasters to recognize their responsibility to frame codes of ethics in concert with their employees to serve as guidelines in furthering these goals.

(Used with permission of SPJ.)

Code of Broadcast News Ethics for the
Radio-Television News Directors Association

RTNDA
1000 Connecticut Ave., Suite 615
Washington, DC 20036
202-223-4007
rtnda@rtnda.org

The responsibility of radio and television journalists is to gather and report information of importance and interest to the public accurately, honestly and impartially.

The members of the Radio-Television News Directors Association accept these standards and will:

1. Strive to present the source or nature of broadcast news material in a way that is balanced, accurate and fair.

    A. They will evaluate information solely on its merits as news, rejecting sensationalism or misleading emphasis in any form.
    B. They will guard against using audio or video material in a way that deceives the audience.
    C. They will not mislead the public by presenting as spontaneous news any material that is staged or rehearsed.
    D. They will identify people by race, creed, nationality or prior status only when it is relevant.
    E. They will clearly label opinion and commentary.
    F. They will promptly acknowledge and correct errors.

2. Strive to conduct themselves in a manner that protects them from conflicts of interest, real or perceived. They will decline gifts or favors that would influence or appear to influence their judgments.

3. Respect the dignity, privacy and well-being of people with whom they deal.

4. Recognize the need to protect confidential sources. They will promise confidentiality only with the intention of keeping that promise.
5. Respect everyone's right to a fail trial.
6. Broadcast the private transmissions of other broadcasters only with permission.
7. Actively encourage observance of this Code by all journalists, whether members of the Radio-Television News Directors Association or not.   *(Used with permission of RTNDA.)*

Code of Ethics for the Public Relations Society of America

PRSA
33 Irving Place
New York, NY 10003
212-995-2230
hq@prsa.org

These articles have been adopted by the Public Relations Society of America to promote and maintain high standards of public service and ethical conduct among its members:

1. A member shall conduct his or her professional life in accord with the public interest.
2. A member shall exemplify high standards of honesty and integrity while carrying out dual obligations to a client or employer and to the democratic process.
3. A member shall deal fairly with the public, with past or present clients or employers, and with fellow practitioners, giving due respect to the ideal of free inquiry and to the opinions of others.
4. A member shall adhere to the highest standards of accuracy and truth, avoiding extravagant claims or unfair comparisons and giving credit for ideas and words borrowed from others.
5. A member shall not knowingly disseminate false or misleading information and shall act promptly to correct erroneous communications for which he or she is responsible.
6. A member shall not engage in any practice that has the purpose of corrupting the integrity of channels of communications or the processes of government.
7. A member shall be prepared to identify publicly the name of the client or employer on whose behalf any public communication is made.

8. A member shall not use any individual or organization professing to serve or represent an announced cause, or professing to be independent or unbiased, but actually serving another or undisclosed interest.

9. A member shall not guarantee the achievement of specified results beyond the member's direct control.

10. A member shall not represent conflicting or competing interests without the express consent of those concerned, given after a full disclosure of the facts.

11. A member shall not place himself or herself in a position where the member's personal interest is or may be in conflict with an obligation to an employer or client, or others, without full disclosure of such interests to all involved.

12. A member shall not accept fees, commissions, gifts or any other consideration from anyone except clients or employers for whom services are performed without their express consent, given after full disclosure of the facts.

13. A member shall scrupulously safeguard the confidences and privacy rights of present, former, and prospective clients or employers.

14. A member shall not intentionally damage the professional reputation or practice of another practitioner.

15. If a member has evidence that another member has been guilty of unethical, illegal, or unfair practices, including those in violation of this Code, the member is obligated to present the information promptly to the proper authorities of the Society for action in accordance with the procedure set forth in Article XII of the Bylaws.

16. A member called as witness in a proceeding for enforcement of this Code is obligated to appear, unless excused for sufficient reason by the judicial panel.

17. A member shall, as soon as possible, sever relations with any organization or individual if such relationship requires conduct contrary to the articles of this Code.

(Used with permission of PRSA.)

Code of Ethics for the National Press Photographers Association

NPPA
3200 Croasdaile Dr., Suite 306
Durham, NC 27705
919-383-7246
nppa@mindspring.com

The National Press Photographers Association, a professional society dedicated to the advancement of photojournalism, acknowledges concern and respect for the public's natural-law right to freedom in searching for the truth and the right to be informed truthfully and completely about public events and the world in which we live.

We believe that no report can be complete if it is not possible to enhance and clarify the meaning of words. We believe that pictures, whether used to depict news events as they actually happen, illustrate news that has happened or to help explain anything of public interest, are an indispensable means of keeping people accurately informed; that they help all people, young and old, to better understand any subject in the public domain.

Believing the foregoing, we recognize and acknowledge that photojournalists should at all times maintain the highest standards of ethical conduct in serving the public interest. To that end the National Press Photographers Association sets forth the following Code of Ethics which is subscribed to by all of its members:

1. The practice of photojournalism, both as a science and art, is worthy of the very best thought and effort of those who enter into it as a profession.

2. Photojournalism affords an opportunity to serve the public that is equaled by few other vocations, and all members of the profession should strive by example and influence to maintain high standards of ethical conduct free of mercenary considerations of any kind.

3. It is the individual responsibility of every photojournalist at all times to strive for pictures that report truthfully, honestly and objectively.

4. Business promotion in its many forms is essential, but untrue statements of any nature are not worthy of a professional photojournalist, and we severely condemn any such practice.

5. It is our duty to encourage and assist all members of our profession, individually and collectively, so that the quality of photojournalism may constantly be raised to higher standards.

6. It is the duty of every photojournalist to work to preserve all freedom-of-the-press rights recognized by law and to work to protect and expand freedom-of-access to all sources of news and visual information.

7. Our standards of business dealings, ambitions and relations shall have in them a note of sympathy for our common humanity and shall always require us to take into consideration our highest duties as

members of society. In every situation in our business life, in every responsibility that comes before us, our chief thought shall be to fulfill that responsibility and discharge that duty so that when each of us is finished, we shall have endeavored to lift the level of human ideals and achievement higher than we found it.

8. No Code of Ethics can prejudge every situation, thus common sense and good judgment are required in applying ethical principles.

(Used with permission of NPPA.)

Laws Useful to Journalists

The First Amendment to the Constitution of the United States

Congress shall make no law respecting an establishment of religion or prohibiting the free exercise thereof; or abridging the freedom of speech, or of the press; or the right of people peaceably to assemble, and to petition the Government for a redress of grievances.

Equal Pay Act of 1963

. . . as amended by the Higher education Act in 1974, prohibits discrimination in salaries, including almost all fringe benefits, on the basis of sex.

Civil Rights Act of 1964

Title VI

". . . no person in the United States shall; on the ground of race, color, or national origin, be excluded from participation in, be denied the benefits of, or be otherwise subjected to discrimination under any program or activity receiving Federal financial assistance . . ." This covers health, welfare, education and others.

Title VII

. . . as amended by the Equal Employment Opportunity Act of 1972, prohibits discrimination in employment including hiring, upgrading, salaries, fringe benefits, training and other conditions of employment.

Higher Education Act 1972

Title IX

. . . prohibits sex discrimination against students or others in education programs or activities . . . or employment.

Rehabilitation Act of 1973

. . . prohibits discrimination through outside contract, in program participation, and in employment. Persons with Disabilities are those having a physical or mental impairment, having a history of such an impairment, or those regarded as having such impairment.

Freedom of Information Act of 1966
(amended 1975, 5 U.S.C. 552) (Rich, 1994)

The FOIA permits "any person" to request access to public agency records. There are several exceptions such as personnel records and records deemed confidential related to national security. In practice "any person" includes U.S. citizens, permanent resident aliens and foreign nationals, as well as corporations, unincorporated associations, universities, state and local governments and members of Congress.

The FOIA requires an agency to respond to an initial request within 10 working days and to an administrative appeal within 20 working days. The agency may take an additional 10 days to respond in "unusual circumstances." If the agency fails to comply, the requester may seek satisfaction in court.

A letter of request should include the following:

1. "This request is made under the Federal Freedom of Information Act, 5 U.S.C. 552."
2. Clearly describe the material you need by giving names, places and period of time about which you are inquiring. You may attach any document that describes the materials you are seeking.
3. Ask the agency to justify any deletions.
4. Because the FOIA waives any copy fee if disclosure could be considered as "primarily benefiting the general public," ask for exemption of fee.
5. Ask them to please respond by 10 business days as required by law.

Age Discrimination in Employment Act of 1975

. . . covers people aged 40 to 70. An employer of more than 20 people cannot discriminate on the basis of age unless age is a bona fide occupational qualification, which is rare. Employers may not advertise so as to indicate a preference or limitation on age, discriminate in hiring on the basis of age; or deny career opportunity on the basis of age.

Americans with Disabilities Act of 1990

. . . no qualified individual with a disability shall, by reason of such disability, be excluded from the participation in, be denied the benefit of, or be subjected to discrimination in federally funded programs or activities.

Copyright Act of 1978
(amended 1994, U.S.C., Title 17) (Mencher, 1994)

In 1978, a federal copyright law was enacted that eliminated earlier state laws.

The purpose of a copyright is to secure for the creator of the material all the benefits earned by creating it. Copyrights apply to written materials as well as to illustrations, plays, musical works, motion pictures, sound recordings, graphics, sculptures, pantomimes, and dances. The new copyright law protects authors for their lifetime plus 50 years.

If you want to copyright material, print *Copyright 19__* next to the author's name. Write to the Register of Copyrights, Library of Congress, Washington, D.C. 20559 for an application form.

Fair use was established in 1978 and covers purposes of criticism, comment, news reporting, teaching, scholarship or research. This is so because it is not used for profit. Small parts are used, and it does not have an effect on the income earned from the copyright. Use only small parts of materials and always attribute their source.

Of particular interest to journalists are materials taken from the Internet.

Be aware that much of the materials on the Net are reprints from publications and therefore copyrighted. If there is any question, ask for reprint rights. You cannot go wrong if you do this and always attribute sources.

One exception to the above is musical copyright. No part of a musical composition or its lyrics may be used without permission, although most classical music is in the public domain.

Libel and Slander

There are both state and federal laws that deal with libel, although they are not identical. Libel is a published defamatory statement. Slander is a spoken defamatory statement. There is civil libel, which is a suit for damages, and there is criminal libel, which can result in fines or imprisonment. A plaintiff in a libel suit must prove four points:

1. That the statement was published to others by print or broadcast.
2. That the plaintiff is identifiable.
3. That there was actual injury in the form of money losses, defamation of reputation, humiliation, or mental anguish and suffering.
4. That the publisher of the statement was malicious or negligent.

Slander is much like libel except that instead of being written it is spoken. The statement can occur in an informal conversation, in a speech or in a broadcast, and a third party must witness the statement.

Truth is an absolute defense to a charge of defamation, although it may not protect against other charges such as invasion of privacy. Other defenses are: opinion rather than fact, consent of one-time publication, and a report of official proceedings or a public meeting.

Privacy

Although truth is the strongest defense against libel, it is the basis of invasion of privacy suits. By definition, invasion of privacy is said to occur when an individual is exposed to public view and suffers mental distress as a consequence of the publicity. Unlike defamation, which has deep roots in the common law, the right of privacy is a fairly new legal development and one in which there is even less certainty for the reporter than in the area of libel. Even though public figures have less privacy than private individuals, the journalist must be careful with both groups. Four areas of privacy should concern the journalist:

1. Publicity that places a person in a false light in the public.
2. Public disclosure of embarrassing private facts (not in an official document) about an individual.
3. Intrusion into a private area for a story or a picture without permission—eavesdropping or trespassing.
4. Use of a person's name or picture without his or her permission. This applies when the picture is used for commercial purposes, such as advertising or promotion.

Shield Laws

Most states have shield laws that allow journalists to protect their sources. Enforcement of these laws varies from state to state. In some states, journalists are in more danger of being cited for contempt of court. The state journalists' associations are a good source of the rights of journalists through their publications and workshops.

Journalists' notes are usually protected as confidential unless it is a criminal case. The shield law is a helpful successor to the **sunshine law**, which requires public agencies to meet in public unless there is a compelling reason for privacy.

U.S. Immigration Status

Immigration policy and law are governed by the Immigration and Nationality Act (INA). These are complex and changed often. When writing about these, contact a legal professional for updated information.

All persons in the United States have an **immigration status** (Internet Immigration Law Center). These are

1. *U.S. Citizen*—Gained by persons at birth in the United States. It may also be gained by birth to U.S. citizen parents or through naturalization.

2. *Permanent Resident*—An immigrant. Permanent residency gives an alien the right to reside permanently in the United States while maintaining his/her own non-U.S. citizenship. Generally, permanent residents are the only ones eligible for naturalization.

3. *Temporary Resident*—Persons who have allied legalization or amnesty. A temporary resident eventually becomes a permanent resident or loses resident status.

4. *Nonimmigrant*—An alien who comes to the United States temporarily for some purpose such as study, business or tourism. Normally, a nonimmigrant leaves the United States at a determined time, although it is possible to change status while in the United States

5. *Asylee*—A person who has been granted asylum but has not yet been granted permanent residency. The Attorney General determines if a person is a refugee, which is defined as "any person who is outside any country in which such person last habitually resided, and who is unable or unwilling to avail himself or herself of the protection of that country because of persecution on account of race, religion, nationality, membership in a particular social group, or political opinion."

6. *Temporary Protected Status*—Persons from designated countries who have been granted the right to remain and work in the United States for a specified time. This is generally due to adverse and extraordinary circumstances in their home country.

7. *Out of Status*—Usually a nonimmigrant who entered the United States with legal status but who has violated the terms of admission, such as overstay.

8. *Undocumented Alien*—Person who has entered the United States illegally, without valid entry status or documentation.

Selected Media and Diversity Organizations

AIDS Action
1875 Connecticut Ave., NW #700
Washington, DC 20009
202-986-1300
www.aidsaction.org

Anti-Defamation League (ADL)
823 United Nations Plaza
New York, NY 10017
212-885-7700
www.adl.org

American Association of Retired Persons (AARP)
601 E. Street, NW
Washington, D.C. 20049
800-424-3410
www.aarp.org

American Society of Newspaper Editors (ASNE)
11690B Sunrise Valley Dr.
Reston, VA 20191-1409
703-453-1122
www.asne.org

Asian American Journalists' Association (AAJA)
1765 Sutter St., Suite 1000
San Francisco, CA 94115
415-346-2051
www.aaja.org

Gay and Lesbian Alliance Against Defamation (GLAAD)
1360 Mission St., Suite 200
San Francisco, CA 94103
415-861-2244
www.glaad.org

Investigative Reporters & Editors (IRE)
University of Missouri School of Journalism
138 Neff Annex
Columbia, MO 65211
573-882-2042
www.ire.org

National Association of Black Journalists (NABJ)
8701A Adelphi Road
Adelphi, MD 20783-1716
301-445-7100
www.nabj.org

National Association of People with AIDS
1413 K St. N.W./7th Floor
Washington, DC 20005
202-898-0414
www.napwa.org

National Federation of Press Women (NFPW)
P.O. Box 5556
Arlington, VA 22205
800-780-2715
www.nfpw.org

National Association of Hispanic Journalists (NAHJ)
1193 National Press Building
Washington, DC 20045-2100
202-662-7145
www:nahj.org

**National Lesbian and Gay
Journalists Association (NLGJA)**
1718 M St., NW #245
Washington, DC 20036
202-588-9888
www.nlgja.org

Native American Journalists Association (NAJA)
1433 E. Franklin Ave., Suite 11
Minneapolis, MN 55404
612-874-8833
www.medill.nwu.edu/naja

Poynter Institute for Media Studies
801 Third St. South

St. Petersburg, FL 33701
813-821-9494
www.poynter.org

The Freedom Forum
1101 Wilson Blvd.
Arlington, VA 22209
703-528-0800
www.newsfreedomforum.org

Internet Resources

Books About Online Usage and Sources

Biagi, Shirley. *Media/Impact, An Introduction to Mass Media* (4th ed.). Belmont, Calif.: Wadsworth Publishing Company, 1999.
Brooks, Brian S. *Journalism in the Information Age: A Guide to Computers for Reporters and Editors.* Boston: Allyn & Bacon, 1997.
Harper, Christopher. *What's Next in Mass Communication: Readings on Media and Culture.* New York: St. Martin's Press, 1998.
Houston, Brant. *Computer-Assisted Reporting: A Practical Guide.* New York: St. Martin's Press, 1996.
Paul, Nora. *Computer Assisted Research: A Guide to Taping Online Information.* St. Petersburg, FL: Poynter Institute for Media Studies, 1996.

Useful Websites

See Chapter 2 for discussion on Computer-Assisted Journalism. Websites and e-mail addresses change often. When you can't connect, use a search engine such as Yahoo to locate your topic.

American Society of Newspaper Editors Minority Employment Report, www.asne.org/kioske/diversity/97/minsrv.htm
Center for Democratic Renewal, "Organizations Responding to Hate Violence," www.publiceye.org/pra/cdr.html
Computer Assisted Reporting, www.home.att.net/-bdedman/index.html
Diversity in Electronic Media, www.mediaaccess.org/program/diversity/
Editor & Publisher Interactive, www.mediainfo.com

FedWorld, www.fedworld.gov

Ford Foundation's Campus Diversity Initiative, www.inform.umd.edu/ diversityweb

Internet News Bureau, www.newsbureau.com

Journalism Related Jobs, http:www.journ.latech.edu.jobs/ jobs_home.html

Library of Congress, //thomas.loc.gov

National Institute for Computer-Assisted Reporting (IRE/NICAR), www.ire.org

Poynter Online, www.poynter.org/research/reshotres.htm

SFSU Center for Integration and Improvement of Journalism, www.journalism.sfsu.edu/www/ciij/rolodex.html

The Beat Page, www.reporter.org/beat/lists.html

U.S. Census Bureau, www.census.gov

Virtual Media Library, www.cais.com/makulow/rlj/html
(A Virtual Gold Mine!)

Hate Groups in America
(Summary from the Anti-Defamation League, 1996)

Violence-Prone Organizations

Ku Klux Klan—An anti-black, anti-Semitic, anti-immigrant, violent movement dating back to post-Civil War days. There are a number of competing Klan organizations with different leaders, but all have the same basic beliefs and use the same trappings of hoods, robes and rituals.

Neo-Nazis—An anti-Semitic, anti-black, anti-immigrant group that patterns itself on the philosophy of Nazi Germany. The various neo-Nazi factions, the largest of which is the New Order, wear Nazi uniforms and regalia.

Aryan Nations—Based in the American Northwest, this is a militant group promoting anti-Semitism, white supremacy and the establishment of a white racist state through a pseudotheology called "Identity." The "Identity" movement holds that white "Aryans," not Jews, are the Biblical "chosen people." Hatred toward nonwhite races and relentless vilification of Jews are major components of the "Identity" movement's ideology.

Skinheads—Gangs of shaven-headed youths, often sporting Nazi insignia, who espouse anti-Semitic and white supremacy. Many members have engaged in violence against blacks, Jews and other minorities. Skinheads have been linked to several organized hate groups, many of whose leaders have targeted them for recruitment. (Note that not all youngsters who adopt the Skinhead style are racists and neo-Nazis.)

White Aryan Resistance (WAR)—A white supremacist group headed by Tom Metzger of California. Metzger's influence extends well beyond his own group. In the mid-1980s Metzger began producing a videotaped series for cable television titled "Race and Reason." The program features sympathetic interviews with hate group figures and has been aired on public access cable channels in major cities across the country. WAR has been the most active recruiter of Skinheads.

Christian Patriots Defense League—A paramilitary organization, with a "survivalist" ideology, to which it has added anti-black, anti-Semitic, anti-immigrant beliefs. Headquartered in Illinois, it has provided paramilitary training to persons steeped in hate.

Propaganda Organizations

National Caucus of Labor Committees (NCLC)—An extremist group whose political arm was the now defunct U.S. Labor Party. It is headed by Lyndon H. LaRouche, Jr., whose conspiracy-oriented writings accuse various governments, groups and prominent individuals of sinister and illegal plots to manipulate political, economic and social events. The group's publications have frequently promoted anti-Semitic views. The NCLC is the nucleus of a group of associated organizations that carry out LaRouche's program. Some of these are the National Democratic Policy Committee, which despite its name has no connection with the Democratic Party; the Fusion Energy Foundation; and the National Anti-Drug Coalition. These groups exploit general public concern over such issues as nuclear energy and drug abuse in order to attract people to LaRouche's extremist beliefs. LaRouche also publicizes his program through the magazine, *Executive Intelligence Review,* and the newspaper, *New Federalist.* Many LaRouche followers have run for office at the local, state and federal levels. LaRouche himself has run for president in 1976, 1980, 1984, and 1988. He has garnered, however, only a minute percentage of the votes cast.

Liberty Lobby—A multi-million-dollar propaganda organization that is the most active anti-Semitic group in the United States Based in Washington, D.C., it publishes a weekly newspaper, *The Spotlight,* that has more than 100,000 subscribers. It has close ties to the Noontide Press, a publisher of pro-Nazi and other extremist books, and to the Institute for Historical Review, a pseudoacademic group, located in Torrance, California, that promotes through publications and conferences, the anti-Semitic theme that the Holocaust is a "hoax."

Liberty Bell Press—A propaganda outfit in West Virginia that publishes and widely disseminates hate literature. It is run by a neo-Nazi who was a member of the Hitler Youth before immigrating to the United States.

National Association for the Advancement of White People (NAAWP)—is a "Klan without robes" that provides an organizational framework through which its leader and founder, former Klan member David Duke, exploits controversial issues such as busing, affirmative action and the financial troubles of U.S. farmers. Promoting itself as a "white rights" lobby, *NAAWP News*, the group's monthly newspaper, regularly publishes articles attacking blacks, Jews and other minorities (Anti-Defamation League, 1996).

Appendix A

―――――――――――◆―――――――

Analyzing a Diversity Article

Stephen T. Magagnini is a veteran reporter at *The Sacramento Bee* in California. He is a graduate of Hampshire College in Massachusetts where he was editor in chief for the campus newspaper. Magagnini has worked for the *San Francisco Chronicle* and the *Sacramento Union* and published in various other prominent newspapers, such as the *Boston Globe,* the *Philadelphia Inquirer* and the *Dallas Times Herald.* He also teaches part-time in the Journalism Division of the Communication Studies Department at California State University, Sacramento.

He is an Asian Studies Fellow of the Freedom Forum Foundation and a Jefferson Fellow in Asian Studies, both at the University of Hawaii. His articles and series have won many journalism awards from media professional groups such as the Society of Professional Journalists, The Newspaper Publishers Association and the San Francisco Press Club.

Magagnini was nominated by *The Bee* for the Pulitzer Prize in 1995 for his coverage of South Africa and for his series on Hmong and Iu Mien shamans, in 1996 for a series "Coming to Sacramento" about the flood of immigrants and refugees to Sacramento, and in 1998 for "Lost Tribes," his series on California Indians. The following is a diversity article, independent of a series.

―――――――――――◆―――――――

"American Indian School
Far From Old 'Institute' Days"

By Stephen Magagnini
Senior Writer for Ethnic Affairs and Race Relations

The Sacramento Bee, February 5, 1997

RIVERSIDE—On a grassy campus here, 450 American Indian teenagers from throughout the United States study basket weaving, tribal government, Navajo and other subjects not found at most public schools.

But Sherman Indian High School is not your ordinary public school. The 105-year-old institution is one of the last vestiges of the old Indian boarding school system—widely considered one of the worst abuses perpetrated against American Indians.

At 10 a.m. today, Sacramento City College will host a Native American Cultural Council forum on Indian boarding schools.

From the 1880s through the 1960s, hundreds of thousands of Indian children across the country were sent to government boarding schools, often hundreds of miles away from home, in an effort to "take the Indian out of the Indian."

Indian children were given haircuts, uniforms, non-Indian names and orders not to speak their native language—even though many arrived not speaking English. Those who violated the English-only rule were often beaten or assigned latrine duty. In the summers they were hired out as domestics or migrant workers.

But the "Sherman Institute" once known for its reform school atmosphere—has undergone a remarkable metamorphosis. Its mission is no longer to eradicate, but to celebrate Indian culture and language.

"We're trying to give back what was taken away," said administrator Ken Taylor, a Creek who attended Haskell, an Indian boarding school in Kansas.

Sherman, which once had 1,200 students, nearly closed in 1992 when local tribes wanted to turn it into an alcohol treatment center. But in the last five years, the school has retrained its teachers to meet the unusual needs of Indian students.

"Man Indian children learn in different ways (than non-Indians) they are visual, hands-on learners; they learn better in groups," said Superintendent Fayetta Babby, a Seneca Cayuga who attended Chilocco Indian School in Oklahoma.

"I was very shy, and it gave me a chance to excel," said Babby, 50. "If not for that experience, I would not be where I am today."

For decades boarding schools were the only way Indians could get a high school education. Indians were not allowed in California's public schools until 1935. The first public high school on the 25,000-square-mile Navajo Reservation didn't open until the 1950s, and by 1955, 81 percent of Navajo children were in boarding schools.

Helen Waukazoo, director of Friendship House, an Indian drug and alcohol treatment program in San Francisco, said she was pulled off the Navajo Reservation at age 8 against her parents' wishes and sent to school in Utah.

"This was another way to disrupt the American Indian Family system," said Waukazoo, 55.

"The only language I knew was Navajo, so I was always punished," she said. "My punishment was to scrub the hallways, windows and floors . . . I couldn't attend any movies or activities."

Indian boarding schools were often at military outposts in isolated areas, where abuses could go unreported. At Stewart Institute in Carson City, which closed in 1980, people have claimed to see the ghosts of Indian children who were sent there and never heard from again.

"This was operated similar to a POW camp when it opened in 1890," said Suzi Lisa, director of the Stewart Cultural Center. "They were innocent victims of a war being waged against them and their culture."

While many Indians in their 40s and 50s forged lifelong friendships and used boarding school as a springboard to decent jobs or college, their parents often endured much harsher treatment. Waukazoo remembers an elderly Indian woman describing how a nun bathed her in water and bleach to try to whiten her brown skin.

Tom Hyde, a Viejas Kummeyaay elder from San Diego, went to Sherman in 1943, then served in World War II. When he and 47 other veterans returned to Sherman, they began to question the teachers.

"They were not qualified—some were matrons out of state prisons and reformatories," said Hyde, who was kicked out for probing teachers' backgrounds.

Hyde said he was recruited for Sherman at 12 by a federal agent who got $125 per child.

Sherman was mostly a trade school, and Hyde spent mornings learning leather work and carpentry. The most important thing he learned, he said, was "responsibility—to keep your word and fulfill your commitments."

Boarding schools were the defining experience for generations of Indians.

"Most reservation Indians over age 30 went to boarding school," said Sherman Museum curator Lorene Sisquoc, who also teaches weaving. "It changed our whole lives."

The nation's 30 off-reservation Indian boarding schools produced thousands of intertribal marriages that spawned generations of mixed-blood Indians.

"There's a lot of bittersweet memories—they tore apart families and some kids never got to go home," Sisquoc said. "You don't know how to function as a family unit." Some elders believe the high rate of Indian domestic abuse can be traced to oppressive boarding school experiences.

After World War II, as a part of the government's push to close reservations and assimilate Indians into "mainstream society," thousands of Indian boarding school grads were funneled into jobs in Los Angeles, San Francisco and other cities.

Today children from 64 tribes attend Sherman, one of five remaining Indian boarding schools. This year, 65 students left because of homesickness, but 90 will graduate and more than a dozen will go on to college.

For information on today's forum, call 558-2155.

Discussion and Questions

1. Write the theme and the purpose of this article, each in one sentence.
2. From reading the article, what was its origin? How did the reporter make it different from others of its kind?
3. How many people did Magagnini quote in the article? What other voices would you like to have heard?
4. Note the many facts and statistics included in the article. Did you learn anything about Indian boarding schools you did not know?
5. What techniques did the reporter use to put you into this culture?

Appendix B

---◆---

Glossary of Terms

Alternate Words and Phrases

The following selected words and phrases do not in any way make up a complete list of the sexist, classist or racist words firmly rooted in the English language. Yet, writers can attempt to clean up those that are recognized.

Some people still use these words and would argue for some of the words on the *THESE COULD OFFEND* list. Ultimately, writers have the responsibility to write as objectively and fairly as possible, not offending those about whom they write.

The point should be made that in conversation and colloquially people use words and phrases that can be considered borderline. Whatever someone says in conversation may be used for quotation if it is relevant and in context for that particular story. But in presenting straight information or even in an opinion piece, writers must be careful. It is prudent for writers to be sensitive to words and phrases not only for civility, but also for the sake of being libel free.

Resources used to compile the following list are located at the end of the References section.

---◆---

THESE COULD OFFEND	*ALTERNATIVES*

A

AIDS victim or AIDS sufferer	person living with AIDS
airman	pilot
all chiefs and no injuns	too many bosses and not enough workers
alumni/alumna	alums, graduates, former students
amputee (disabled)	one who has lost a limb(s)
anchorman	anchor
Anglo	Anglo-American, white
assemblyman, assemblywoman	assembly member
authoress	author

B

babe	an attractive woman
bachelor's degree	undergraduate degree
old bag	an older woman
bag lady	a homeless woman
ball and chain	wife
barrio	poor Hispanic neighborhood
basket case (disabled)	*eliminate*
bastard (classist)	born out of marriage
better half	wife
be your own man	be your own person
beaner	a Mexican, Mexican American
best man for the job	best person for the job
Bible thumper	conservative Christian
bimbo (woman)	*eliminate*
birth defect	born with . . .
blind	visually impaired
blind as a bat	*eliminate*
boy	use for under 18 years; use man for over 18 years
boy friend	friend, companion
brave	a (tribal name) warrior
broad	woman
brotherhood	humanity
buck	a young male
bum	someone without work
businessmen	business people
butch	lesbian

C

canuck	French Canadian
camera girl	photographer
caveman	cave dweller
chairman	chair, chairperson
Chicano	Mexican American
chick	woman
Chinaman, chink	Chinese, Chinese American

not having a Chinaman's chance   not likely
churchman   church member
city slicker   city dweller
cleaning lady   housecleaner, housekeeper
old codger   an older man
coed (woman)   student
colored   a black person
confined to a wheelchair   person who uses a wheelchair
congressman, congresswoman   congress member
coolie   Chinese laborer
councilman, councilwoman   council member
cracker (classist)   *eliminate*
craftsman   skilled worker or crafts worker
crazy   mental disorder
crewman   crew member
cripple (disabled)   one who walks with difficulty
crone (older woman)   *eliminate*

D
dame   woman
dancing girl   dancer
deaconess   deacon
deaf as a doorknob (disabled)   *eliminate*
deaf and dumb   hearing impaired
deaf mute   speech impaired
Dear Sir (letter salutation)   Dear Mr. or Dear Ms.
deformed   one who has a disability
delivery boy   delivery person, deliverer
distaff (women)   *eliminate*
doll (woman)   *eliminate*
dragon lady   *eliminate*
druggie   a drug addict
Dutchman   Dutch citizen
dutch treat   each pays own way
dwarf   little person
dyke   lesbian

E
elderly   older adults
enlisted man   enlistee
Eskimo   Inuk, plural is Inuit
executrix   executor

F
fag or faggot   gay, homosexual male
fairy   gay, homosexual male
fair sex   women
fallen woman   *eliminate*
family of man   humankind or humanity

fatherland	homeland
feebleminded	developmentally disabled
female doctor, lawyer, engineer, etc.	doctor, lawyer, engineer, etc.
feminize	to soften
filly (woman)	*eliminate*
fireman	firefighter
fisherman	fisher
fishwife	a quarrelsome woman
forefathers	ancestors
foreman	supervisor
four-eyes	wears glasses
fraternal twins	nonidentical twins
fraternize	associate
Frenchman	French citizen
freshman	first-year student

G

gentleman	man
gentleman's agreement	honorable agreement
getting senile	age stereotype (unless it is a medical condition)
ghetto	a poor ethnic neighborhood
ghetto blaster	portable stereo
gimp (disabled)	*eliminate*
girl	use for under 18 years; use woman for over 18 years
girl friend	friend, companion
governess	instructor
grandfather clause	escape clause
gringo (white)	*eliminate*
gyped me out of it (Gypsy)	cheated me out of it

H

half-breed	person of mixed heritage
handyman	repair person or repairer
handicapped	disabled or physically challenged
haole	a white person
harelip (disabled)	*eliminate*
hatchet man	hatchet person
headmaster	principal
heiress	heir
henpecked	*eliminate*
heroine	hero
hick	an ignorant person
high class	*describe behavior*
hillbilly	person who lives in Appalachia
honest injun	it's the truth
holy roller	a conservative Christian
honkers	women's breasts
honky	a white person
hooters	women's breasts
homeroom mother	homeroom parent

homo	gay, homosexual male
hostess	host
housewife	homemaker

I

idiot	developmentally disabled
imbecile	developmentally disabled
Indian	tribal name: Navajo, Native American
indian giver	taking something back you have given
Indian maiden	a young Native American woman
injun	give tribal name: a Navajo
illegal alien	undocumented worker
insane (disabled)	mental disorder
invalid	bedridden or house bound

J

Jack of all trades	good at all things
Jap	Japanese
JAP, Jewish American princess	*eliminate*
Jesus freak	a conservative Christian
jewed him down (Jewish)	bartered the price down
journeyman	trainee

K

kingpin	top person, leader
kinsman	kin
knockers	women's breasts
Koran	Curan

L

lady	woman
lady luck	luck
lame (disabled)	one who walks with difficulty
landlord	owner
lawman	name position: sheriff, judge, etc.
layman	layperson
in layman's terms	in nontechnical terms
leading lady	lead
left-handed compliment	ambiguous, doubtful
lesbo	lesbian, a homosexual woman
libber	liberationist, feminist
little lady	wife
little woman	wife, woman
low class (classist)	*describe behavior*
low man on the totem pole	last in line
low rider	Mexican youths who drive altered vehicles
lumberman	wood chopper
lush	an alcoholic

M

madam (woman)	*eliminate*
madam chairman	I address the chair
maid	houseworker, room cleaner
maiden lady	single
maiden name	former name
maiden voyage	first voyage
mailman	mail carrier
maintenance man	maintenance person
manhole	maintenance hole
man the stations	take the stations
man-eater	human-eater
manhandle	to handle roughly
manhood	adulthood
man hours	staff hours
manhunt	a search
mankind	humankind
manmade	artificial, synthetic
manning	staffing
man overboard	person overboard
manpower	workforce
man-sized	big, large
manslaughter	human slaughter
man-to-man (sports)	player-to-player
marksman	sharpshooter
master	head, expert
master of ceremonies	leader of ceremonies
mastermind	carry out project skillfully
masterpiece	great work
medicine man	shaman, a healer
Mexican standoff	a standoff
midget	little person
Miss or Mrs.	Ms.
Mongoloid	Mongolian
Moonie	member of the Unification Church
moron	developmentally disabled
Moslem	Muslim
mothering	parenting
Mother Nature	nature
Muhammadan	Muslim
murderess	murderer

N

nanny	nurse
Near East	Middle East
Negro or nigger	black, African American, person of color
newsman	news person
night watchman	night guard
normal	don't use with disabled; use nondisabled

O

okie (geographic)	slang for poor from Oklahoma—*eliminate*
old biddy	older woman
old geezer	older man
old goat	older man
old maid (woman)	single
old wives' tale	folklore, superstition
oldsters	older adults
ombudsman	investigator
one-man show	one-person show
Oriental	Asian, name by country: Japanese

P

paddy wagon (Irish)	police van
papoose	Native American baby
patrolman	patrol officer
patroness	patron
penmanship	handwriting
pig	a law enforcement officer, a sexist man
plain Jane (woman)	*eliminate*
policeman	police officer
project	subsidized housing
proprietress	proprietor

Q

queen	gay, homosexual man
queer	homosexual man or woman

R

raped	only use literally
red man	use tribal name, Native American
redface	use tribal name, Native American
redneck (classist)	one who has ignorant behavior
reformed alcoholic	recovering alcoholic
retard	developmentally disabled
right-hand man	right hand
rug rat	a child

S

saleslady, salesman	salesperson
Scotch	Scottish
seaman	sailor
serviceman	service person, servicer
sexual preference	sexual orientation
shanghai (geographic)	to take someone against their will
showgirl	dancer
shrew (woman)	*eliminate*
Siamese twins (disabled)	joined twins
significant other	partner, companion

worked like a slave	worked hard
slum (geographic)	poor economic area
songstress	singer
sorceress	sorcerer
spase or spastic (disabled)	one who has cerebral palsy
spinster	a single woman
spokesman	speaker
squaw	Native American woman
starlet	star
straight man	straight person
stewardess	flight attendant
suffragette	suffragist

T

tart (woman)	*eliminate*
trailer trash (classist)	*eliminate*
tramp (woman)	*eliminate*
trash (classist)	*eliminate*
tribe	name group: Cherokee Nation
trick	a person who solicits a prostitute
two-man	two-person

U

Uncle Tom (black)	stereotype—*eliminate*
underdeveloped nation	developing nation
unwed mother	mother
usherette	usher

V

vamp (woman)	*eliminate*
vixen (woman)	*eliminate*

W

waitress	waiter, server
warpath	warring
wampum	money
WASP	White Anglo-Saxon Protestant
weaker sex (women)	*eliminate*
weathergirl	weather reporter
welsh on a promise (Welsh)	not keep a promise
wetback	Mexican laborer
wheelchair bound (disabled)	uses a wheelchair
whore (woman)	a female prostitute
wimp	a weak person

Y

yes man	yes person

References

---◆---

Chapter 1

AIDS Hotline. 800-342-AIDS, 24-hour service through the Centers for Disease Control and Prevention, Atlanta, Ga., May 20, 1996.

Alim, Fahizah. "Too much pain behind one word," *The Sacramento Bee*, Feb. 7, 1994.

American Society of Newspaper Editors. *Covering the Community*. Reston, Va.: ASNE, 1993.

Brooks, Brian S., James L. Pinson and Jean Gaddy Wilson. *Working With Words* (third edition). New York: St. Martin's Press, 1997.

Gersh, Debra. "Covering the Total Community," *Editor & Publisher*, May 15, 1993.

Goldstein, Norm, ed. *The Associated Press Stylebook and Libel Manual*. New York: Associated Press, 1998.

Hussey, Elaine T. *Valuing Workforce Diversity*. Sacramento, Calif.: Affirmative Action Office of the California Energy Commission, 1994.

Kemp, Evan J., chairman U.S. Equal Employment Opportunity Commission. "Have Civil Rights Become Group Rights?" Speech before the National Press Club, Washington, D.C., Nov. 24, 1992.

Nakamura, David. sports writer for *The Washington Post*, interview in Washington, D. C., Nov. 1, 1995.

New York Times/Washington. "Taking bias out of sign language." Reprinted by *The Sacramento Bee*, Jan. 3, 1994.

News Watch: A Critical Look at Coverage of People of Color. San Francisco: Center for Integration and Improvement of Journalism, San Francisco State University, a Unity Project, 1994.

Richburg, Keith B. *Out of America*. New York: HarperCollins, 1997.

Sass, Gerald M., senior vice president of The Freedom Forum. Speech before the National Association of Black Journalists, Atlanta, Ga., July 28, 1994.

Savage, David G. "Minorities press for newsroom diversity," *Los Angeles Times*, July 27, 1994.

Chapter 2

Asian American Journalists Association, *The Asian American Handbook*. Chicago: The National Conference of Christians and Jews and the Chicago Chapter of the Asian American Journalists Association, 1991.

Bee News Service. "Woman backed as prime minister," Bee News Service, Nov. 4, 1997.

Ben, Anna, ed., *Insight Guides Russia*. Boston: Houghton Mifflin, 1995.

DeFao, Janine. "Helping kids dress for success," *The Sacramento Bee*, Nov. 8, 1997.

"Doing ethics in journalism," videotape, St. Petersburg, Fla.: Poynter Institute for Media Studies, 1995.

Garza, Melita. "Handcuffed reporting: Is crime coverage race-based?" *Chicago Tribune*, Unity Conference Panel, July 28, 1994.

Hough, George A. "Reporting and reporters," In *News Writing* (fifth edition). Boston: Houghton Mifflin, 1995, pp. 25-31.

Laakaniemi, Ray. "The nature of news," In *Newswriting in Transition*. Chicago: Nelson-Hall Publishers, 1995, pp. 3-23.

Magagnini, Stephen, senior writer for ethnic affairs and race relations for *The Sacramento Bee*, interview, Sacramento, Calif., Aug. 15, 1997.

Newsday. "Celebrate diversity," *Newsday*, Internet, Aug. 16, 1997.

Chapter 3

American Society of Newspaper Editors Minorities Committee. *The Multicultural Newsroom: How to Get the Best from Everybody*. Reston, Va.: ASNE, 1993-94.

Asian American Journalists Association, *The Asian American Handbook*. Chicago: The National Conference of Christians and Jews and the Chicago Chapter of the Asian American Journalists Association, 1991.

Associated Press Atlanta. "Native American group plans to organize protest during world series," Associated Press Atlanta, Oct. 24, 1995.

Bernstein, Carl. Speech at the 50th Anniversary Gala, Boston University, Sept. 20, 1997.

Clark, Don. "Spanish-language thesaurus has red-faced microsoft somewhat tongue-tied," *The Wall Street Journal*, July 8, 1996.

Ellis, Claire. *Culture Shock! A Guide to Customs and Etiquette, Vietnam*. Portland, Ore.: Graphic Arts Center Publishing, 1995.

"Doing ethics in journalism," videotape, St. Petersburg, Fla.: Poynter Institute for Media Studies, 1995.

Graham, Brad. "Media Diversity," panel at the Multicultural Journalism Association. St. Louis, Mo., Feb. 23, 1996.

Laakaniemi, Ray. *Newswriting in Transition*. Chicago: Nelson-Hall Publishers, 1995.

Lanson, Gerald and Mitchell Stephens. *Writing and Reporting the News* (second edition). New York: Harcourt Brace College Publishers, 1994.

Lippman, Thomas W., ed., *The Washington Post Deskbook on Style*. New York: McGraw-Hill, 1989.

Lynch, Stephen. "The great equalizer," Knight-Ridder News Service, Sept. 17, 1997.

Mead, Tyra. "Navato police probe assault on student," *San Francisco Chronicle,* March 24, 1995.

Media Report to Women. "Minnesota women's press finds women only 25% of names in news," *Media Report to Women.* p. 3, Vol. 26, No. 2, Spring 1998.

Newsday. "Celebrate diversity: People in the news," *Newsday,* Internet, Aug. 16, 1997.

Page, Clarence. "N-Word will sting . . . if you let it," *Chicago Tribune.* Reprinted in *The Sacramento Bee,* Oct. 16, 1997.

Paul, Nora. *Computer Assisted Research: A Guide to Tapping Online Information* (third edition). St. Petersburg, Fla.: Poynter Institute for Media Studies, 1996.

Powell, Adam Clayton, III. "Diversity in Cyberspace" speech of the Freedom Forum Media Studies Center. AEJMC convention in Washington, D.C., Aug. 10, 1995.

Spohn, Michael. "Panel discusses media diversity," *The Maneater.* Columbia, Mo., Feb. 23, 1996.

Ullmann, John. *Investigative Reporting.* New York: St. Martin's Press, 1995.

Chapter 4

Acker, David D. *Skill in Communication* (second edition). Fort Belvoir, Va.: Defense Systems Management College, 1992.

Biagi, Shirley. *Interviews That Work* (second edition). Belmont, Calif.: Wadsworth Publishing, 1992.

"Doing ethics in journalism," videotape, St. Petersburg, Fla.: Poynter Institute for Media Studies, 1995.

Fedler, Fred. *Reporting for the Print Media* (fifth edition). New York: Harcourt Brace Jovanovich, 1993.

Gaines, William. *Investigative Reporting for Print and Broadcast.* Chicago: Nelson-Hall Publishers, 1994.

Goldstein, Norm, ed. *The Associate Press Stylebook and Libel Manual* (sixth edition). New York: Addison-Wesley, 1996.

Keir, Gerry, Maxwell McCombs and Donald L. Shaw. *Advanced Reporting: Beyond News Events.* Prospect Heights, Ill.: Waveland Press, 1991.

Laakaniemi, Ray. *Newswriting in Transition.* Chicago: Nelson-Hall Publishers, 1995.

Lathrop, Douglas. "Challenging Perceptions," *The Quill,* July/August 1995.

Metzler, Ken. *Creative Interviewing* (second edition). Englewood Cliffs, N.J.: Prentice Hall, 1989.

Mitchell, Catherine C. and Mark D. West. *The News Formula.* New York: St. Martin's Press, 1996.

Moon, Jade, news anchor KGMB-TV, Channel 9, interview, Honolulu, Hawaii, Jan. 27, 1996.

Rich, Carole. *Writing and Reporting News.* Belmont, Calif.: Wadsworth Publishing, 1994.

Ullmann, John. *Investigative Reporting.* New York: St. Martin's Press, 1995.

Weinberg, Steve. *The Reporter's Handbook.* New York: St. Martin's Press, 1996.

Chapter 5

Alim, Fahizah. "What's in a word? The N word?" *The Sacramento Bee,* Feb. 7, 1994.

Baldridge, Charlene. "Rededication," Copley News Service. Reprinted in "Countdown to Christmas," *The Sacramento Bee,* Dec. 18, 1997, p. 11.

Bernstein, Carl. Speech at the 50th Anniversary Gala, Boston University, Sept. 20, 1997.

Black, Jay, Bob Steele and Ralph Barney. *Doing Ethics in Journalism.* Boston: Allyn & Bacon, 1995.

Buchanan, Edna. *The Corpse Had a Familiar Face.* New York: Random House, 1987, p. 10.

Cappon, Rene J. *The Word: The Associated Press Guide to Good News Writing.* New York: Associated Press, 1984.

Charlton, James, ed. *The Writer's Quotation Book.* New York: Penguin Books, 1986, p. 41.

Cheney, Theodore A. Rees. *Writing Creative Nonfiction.* Berkeley, Calif.: Ten Speed Press, 1991.

Fitzhenry, Robert I., ed., *The Harper Book of Quotations* (third edition). New York: Harper Perennial, 1993.

Fry, Don, ed., *1993 Best Newspaper Writing.* St. Petersburg, Fla.: Poynter Institute for Media Studies, 1993.

Hall, Donald. *Writing Well* (sixth edition). Glenview, Ill.: Scott, Foresman, 1988.

Harper, Timothy. "Setting the Record Straight," *Sky,* January 1998, pp. 68-73.

Hemingway, Ernest. *In Our Time.* New York: Charles Scribner's Sons, 1935, p. 23.

"Hemingway Quotes," Internet, www.casess.unt.edu/palmer/hemingwa.htm, April 2, 1997.

Hunt, Albert R., executive editor for the Washington, D.C. bureau of *The Wall Street Journal* and *Dow Jones,* Award of Excellence speech at the University of South Dakota, Nov. 15, 1995.

KRON-TV, NewsCenter 4, San Francisco, 1998.

Kurtz, Howard. *Media Circus: The Trouble With America's Newspapers.* New York: Time Books, 1994, chap. 15, pp. 355-378.

Lewis, Alec, compiler. *The Quotable Quotations Book.* New York: Thomas Y. Crowell, Publishers, 1980, p. 306.

Renault, Dennis. Editorial page cartoon, *The Sacramento Bee,* Feb. 4, 1994.

Seigenthaler, John, chairman of The Freedom Forum First Amendment Center in Nashville, Tenn., "What Should Journalists Be Learning?" speech at The Freedom Forum Newsroom Training Conference, Aug. 7, 1995.

Writer's Digest. "206 Tips from Writers," In *The Basics of Writing Bestsellers.* Cincinnati, Ohio: Writer's Digest, Vol. 17, 1995.

Chapter 6

American Society of Newspaper Editors. "The Changing Face of the Newsroom," *ASNE Report.* Washington, D.C.: ASNE, 1988.

Associated Press. "Photo Captions," In *The Associated Press Stylebook and Libel Manual,* New York: Associated Press, 1984.

"Cartoon on racism is still controversial," *Editor & Publisher,* Nov. 16, 1995.

"Doing Ethics in Journalism, Decision-Making in the Newsroom and in the Field," videotape, St. Petersburg, Fla.: The Poynter Institute for Media Studies, 1995.

Hirt, Jane. "Paper's cartoon angers black leaders," *Chicago Tribune*, Nov. 24, 1995.

Irby, Kenneth F., photojournalist and associate at Poynter Institute for Media Studies, interview, Washington, D.C., Nov. 1, 1995.

Leo, John. "Society," *U.S. News & World Report*, Online, Internet, webmaster@us-news.com, 1997.

Lester, Paul Martin, ed., "Images that Heal," by J. B. Colson. In *Images that Injure*. Westport, Conn: Praeger, 1996, chap. 33, pp. 215-236.

——. "Media Victims," by James W. Brown, chap.32, p. 205-214.

Lorenzo, Paula. "Letters to the Editor," *The Sacramento Bee*, March 2, 1996.

McCain, Nina. "Cartoonists deny any ethical bias," *The Boston Globe*, Aug. 31, 1980.

Miller, John and Kimberly Price. "The Imperfect Mirror: Analysis on Minority Pictures & News in Six Canadian Newspapers," Ryerson School of Journalism, 1994.

Moeller, Susan D. "Dangerous Exposures," *Media Studies Journal*, Fall 1996.

Morris, John G. *Get the Picture*. New York: Random House, 1998, p. 268.

Nauman, Art. "Beetle Bailey Gets Sensitive," *The Sacramento Bee*, June 29, 1997.

News Watch: A Critical Look at Coverage of People of Color. San Francisco: Center for Integration and Improvement of Journalism, San Francisco State University, A Unity Project, 1994.

"Visualizing the News," *Newsweek*. Department/Bylines, Online, Internet, April 14, 1997.

Chapter 7

"Celebrity Culture Sinks Politics Again," *MediaWatch*, Vol. 11, Issue 10, Oct. 1997.

"Choice Champions," *New Choices*, Part 10 of a series, Dec. 1994/Jan. 1995.

Chronkite, Walter. *A Reporter's Life*. New York: Ballantine, 1996, p. 382.

Cohler, David Keith. "Is a Picture Worth a Thousand Words?" In *Broadcast Journalism, A Guide for the Presentation of Radio and Television News*. Englewood Cliffs, N.J.: Prentice Hall, 1994, chap. 14, pp. 192-202.

Cohler, David Keith. "Writing for the Ear," *Broadcast Newswriting*. Englewood Cliffs, N.J.: Prentice Hall, 1990, chap. 1, pp. 1-9.

Corliss, Richard. "Look who's talking," *Time*, America on Line, Oct. 13, 1995.

Craft, Christine, "Tuned out," *Sacramento News and Review*, May 23, 1996.

"Diversity channel," *Shirley Biagi's Media/Impact Update*. Belmont, Calif.: Wadsworth Publishing, Fall 1995.

Frankel, Bruce. "Stern tries to soothe Hispanics," *USA TODAY*, April 7, 1995.

Heider, Don. "Ethnic culture and television news: An ethnographic study of Hispanic journalists," Boulder: University of Colorado, 1994.

Hyman, Valerie, director of the Broadcast Journalists' Program, Poynter Institute for Media Studies. "Getting more diversity in content." St. Petersburg, Fla.: Poynter Institute Online, Internet, March 1996.

——. "Power Reporting."

——. "Toward Enterprise Reporting."

"Is Tiger Woods Redefining Race, Too?" *Newsweek*. Departments/My Turn, Online, America on Line, May 12, 1997.

Ivins, Molly. "Lyin' bully," *Mother Jones*, June-July, 1995.

Leonard, John. *Smoke & Mirrors*. New York: The New Press, 1997, p. 265.

Mann, Rick. "Author to discuss father of hate radio: radio priest," news release, University of Missouri-Kansas City, Nov. 8, 1997.

Moon, Jade, news anchor for KGMB-TV 9 (CBS affiliate), interview, Honolulu, Hawaii, Jan. 27, 1996.

NBC, Access Hollywood, Internet, Nov. 26, 1997.

Orlik, Peter B. *Broadcast/Cable Copywriting* (fifth edition). Boston: Allyn & Bacon, 1994.

Roberts, Cokie, ABC news correspondent, "Diversity, Caring Needed in Newsrooms" speech accepting Award for Excellence in Journalism, University of South Dakota in Vermillion, Oct. 2, 1997.

"Single standard on bigotry needed: WABC hate warrants scrutiny," FAIR, Internet, Oct. 25, 1994.

Stephens, Mitchell. "Writing to visuals," In *Broadcast News*. New York: Harcourt Brace Jovanovich College Publishers, 1993. chap. 16, pp. 380-403.

Trahant, Mark N. "Giving native Alaskans a media voice," New America News Service, April 24, 1995.

Webster, Daniel, WTVT-TV news director, videotape, "Doing Ethics in Journalism, Decision-making in the Newsroom and in the Field." St. Petersburg, Fla.: Poynter Institute for Media Studies, 1995.

Woodruff, Judy, television journalist, speech to faculty and students at the University of South Dakota, Nov. 15, 1995.

Chapter 8

Acker, David D. *Skill in Communication* (second edition). Washington, D.C.: Superintendent of Documents, 1992.

Balmaseda, Liz. "Discrimination takes many forms, but not a Chihuahua's," Knight Ridder/Tribune Information Services, May 21, 1998.

Biagi, Shirley and Marilyn Kern-Foxworth, eds., "Public Relations: an Opportunity to Influence the Media," In *Facing Difference*. Thousand Oaks, Calif.: Pine Forge Press, 1997, chap. 4-5, pp. 166-172.

Christians, Clifford G., Mark Fackler and Kim B. Rotzoll. "Persuasion and Advertising," In *Media Ethics* (fourth edition). New York: Longman Publishers, 1995, pp. 133-222.

——. "Persuasion and Public Relations," pp. 223-257.

Clark, Eric. "Advertising and the Media," In *The Want Makers*. New York: Penguin Books, 1990, chap. 10, pp. 317-170.

Copeland, Tara. "Kilbourne blames advertising for negative view of women," *Paladin*. Furman University, Internet, April 15, 1996.

"Designer Hilfiger disputes Net rumors of racism," *USA TODAY*, Internet, Sept. 2, 1997.

Enrico, Dottie. "Milk mustache ads tickle consumers," *USA TODAY*, Nov. 3, 1997.

Hafer, W. Keith and Gordon E. White. "What Makes Good Advertising and Good Advertising Writers," In *Advertising Writing* (third edition). New York: West Publishing Company, 1988, chap. 1, p. 2.

Hershey, Laura. "False advertising: Let's stop the pity campaigns for people with disabilities," *Ms*, March/April 1995, p. 96.

Kirkpatrick, John. "Advertising aimed at Latino market soars," Knight Ridder Newspapers, Jan. 23, 1998.

"Language translations can create new meaning," *Funny Times*, March 1995.

Marlowe, Gene. "Watching TV can cost you a lot more than time," Scripps Howard News Service, June 11, 1998.

Neergaard, Lauran. "Secret documents reveal marketing strategy papers: RJR targeted teens," Associated Press, Internet, Jan. 14, 1998.

"Reebok stumbles badly with DMX," *Los Angeles Times*, Nov. 13, 1997.

Chapter 9

American Society of Newspaper Editors. *Covering the Community: Newspaper Content Audits*. Reston, Va.: ASNE, 1993.

American Society of Newspaper Editors. *The Multicultural Newsroom: How to Get the Best from Everybody*. Reston, Va.: ASNE, 1993.

American Society of Newspaper Editors. *Reporting on People with Disabilities*. ASNE Disabilities Committee Report, Washington, D.C.: ASNE, 1990.

Asian American Handbook. Chicago: The National Conference of Christians and Jews and the Asian American Journalists Association, Chicago Chapter, 1991. (NCCJ, 360 N. Michigan Ave., Suite 1009, Chicago, IL 60601-3803)

Axtell, Roger E., ed., *Do's and Taboos Around the World* (third edition). New York: John Wiley, 1993.

Benn, Anna, ed., *Russia, Insight Guide*. Boston: Houghton, Mifflin, 1995.

Cullen, Kit, former commissioner for Sacramento County Commission on Aging, interview, Sacramento, Calif., April 16, 1996.

Dalton, Larry, freelance photojournalist, interview, Sacramento, Calif., Oct. 12, 1994.

Ellis, Claire. *Culture Shock! Vietnam*. Portland, Ore.: Graphic Arts Center Publishing Co., 1995.

Featherstone, Elena, writer and film maker, "Sex, Lies & Stereotypes: Images of People of Color in the Media" speech at CSUS, Sacramento, Calif., Feb. 2, 1995.

Gerhardt, Dr. Ann L., president of Women Insisting on Natural Shapes (WINS), "Realities of Women," speech to AAUW, Sacramento, Calif., Nov. 16, 1995.

Image of Women in Television: A study. Sacramento, Calif.: American Association of University Women, 1974.

Irby, Kenneth, photojournalist and associate at Poynter Institute for Media Studies, interview, Washington, D.C., Nov. 2, 1995.

Keen, Lisa M. "6 Tips to Help Modernize Gay-Related Coverage," *ASNE Bulletin*, 1987.

Mitchell, Joyce, independent TV producer and AIDS reporter, interview, Sacramento, Calif., April 4, 1998.

Moon, Jade, news anchor, KGMB-TV, Channel 9, interview, Honolulu, Hawaii, Jan. 26, 1996.

Nakamura, David, sports reporter, *Washington Post,* interview, Washington, D.C., Nov. 2, 1995.

Ramos, George, *Los Angeles Times,* senior writer for Latino affairs, interview on Tom Leykas Show, KSTE-Radio, Los Angeles, March 13, 1996.

Takaki, Ronald. *A Different Mirror: A History of Multicultural America.* Boston: Little, Brown & Co., 1993.

Thomas, Helen, correspondent, United Press International, "Women in the Media" speech to the College Media Conference, Washington, D.C. Nov. 3, 1995.

Trask, Lisa, R.N. Director of the University of California, Davis Medical Center Elderly Care Management Program, interview, Sacramento, Calif., April 3, 1998.

Chapter 10

Anti-Defamation League. *Extremist Groups in the United States.* New York: AFL (1996 catalogue).

Black, Jay, Bob Steele and Ralph Barney. *Doing Ethics in Journalism.* Boston: Allyn & Bacon, 1995.

DuBoff, Leonard D. *The Law (In Plain English) for Writers.* Seattle: Madrona Press, 1987.

Houston, Brant. *Computer-Assisted Reporting.* New York: St. Martin's Press, 1996.

Humphrey, Dr. Robert, media law professor, Communication Studies Dept., California State University, Sacramento, interview, April 11, 1996.

Hussey, Elaine T. *Valuing Workforce Diversity.* Sacramento, Calif.: California Energy Commission, 1994.

Internet Immigration Law Center, Immlaw1@aol.com. U.S. Department of Health and Human Services, Office for Civil Rights, Washington, D.C. 20201.

Mencher, Melvin. *News Reporting and Writing* (sixth edition). Madison, Wisconsin: WCB Brown & Benchmark Publishers, 1994.

Rich, Carole. *Writing and Reporting the News.* Belmont, Calif.: Wadsworth Publishing Company, 1994.

Wilcox, Dennis L. and Lawrence W. Nolte. *Public Relations Writing and Media Techniques.* New York: Harper and Row, 1990.

Resources

American Association of University Women Media Committee. *The Image of Women in Television.* Sacramento, California: AAUW, 1974.

American Society for Public Administration, National Committee on Women. *The Right Word: Guidelines for Avoiding Sex-Biased Language.* Washington, D.C.: ASPA, 1979.

Brooks, Brian S., James L. Pinson and Jean Gaddy Wilson. *Working with Words: A Concise Handbook for Media Writers and Editors.* New York: St. Martin's, 1997.

Bunker, Dusty. *Broads and Narrows: A Thinking Wo/man's Dictionary.* Exeter, N.H.: self-published, 1987.

Disabilities Committee of the American Society of Newspaper Editors. *Reporting on People with Disabilities*. Washington, D.C.: ASNE, 1990.

Fergusson, Rosalind. From the works of Eric Partridge and Paul Beal, *Shorter Dictionary of Catch Phrases*. London: Routledge, 1994.

Freeman, G. "What's in a Name?" *The Quill,* May 1991.

Kessler, Lauren and Duncan McDonald. *When Words Collide,* fourth edition. Belmont, Calif.: Wadsworth, 1996.

Literacy Committee of the American Society of Newspaper Editors. *Ways with Words*. Reston, Va.:ASNE Foundation, 1992.

Maggio, Rosalie. *The Nonsexist Word Finder: A Dictionary of Gender-Free Usage*. Boston: Beacon, 1988.

Martindale, C. "Coverage of Black Americans in Four Major Newspapers, 1950-1989," *Newspaper Research Journal,* Summer, pp. 96-111.

Miller, Casey and Kate Swift. *The Handbook of Nonsexist Writing for Writers, Editors and Speakers*. New York: Lippincott & Crowell, 1980.

Parrillo, Vincent N. *Diversity in America*. Thousand Oaks, Calif.: Pine Forge, 1996.

Schwartz, Marilyn and Task Force on Bias-Free Language. *Guidelines for Bias-Free Writing*. Bloomington, Ind.: Association of American University Presses, 1995.

Sorrels, Bobbye D. *The Nonsexist Communicator*. Englewood Cliffs, N.J.: Prentice Hall, 1983.

Index